DOWN
AROUND
MIDNIGHT

DOWN
AROUND
MIDNIGHT

A Memoir of Crash and Survival

ROBERT SABBAG

VIKING

VIKING
Published by the Penguin Group
Penguin Group (USA) Inc., 375 Hudson Street, New York, New York 10014, U.S.A.
Penguin Group (Canada), 90 Eglinton Avenue East, Suite 700, Toronto, Ontario,
Canada M4P 2Y3 (a division of Pearson Penguin Canada Inc.)
Penguin Books Ltd, 80 Strand, London WC2R 0RL, England
Penguin Ireland, 25 St Stephen's Green, Dublin 2, Ireland
(a division of Penguin Books Ltd)
Penguin Books Australia Ltd, 250 Camberwell Road, Camberwell, Victoria 3124,
Australia (a division of Pearson Australia Group Pty Ltd)
Penguin Books India Pvt Ltd, 11 Community Centre, Panchsheel Park,
New Delhi – 110 017, India
Penguin Group (NZ), 67 Apollo Drive, Rosedale, North Shore 0632, New Zealand
(a division of Pearson New Zealand Ltd)
Penguin Books (South Africa) (Pty) Ltd, 24 Sturdee Avenue, Rosebank,
Johannesburg 2196, South Africa

Penguin Books Ltd, Registered Offices: 80 Strand, London WC2R 0RL, England

First published in 2009 by Viking Penguin, a member of Penguin Group (USA) Inc.

1   3   5   7   9   10   8   6   4   2

Copyright © Robert Sabbag, 2009
All rights reserved

LIBRARY OF CONGRESS CATALOGING-IN-PUBLICATION DATA
Sabbag, Robert.
Down around midnight a plane crash and its aftermath / by Robert Sabbag.
p. cm.
ISBN 978-0-670-02102-4
1. Sabbag, Robert.   2. Aircraft accident victims—United States—Biography.
3. Authors—United States—Biography.   4. Survival after airplane
accidents, shipwrecks, etc.   5. Aircraft accidents—Massachusetts—Cape
Cod Region.   I. Title.
TL553.9.S33   2009
363.12'4092—dc22
[B]   2008046688

Printed in the United States of America

To Patricia

DOWN
AROUND
MIDNIGHT

The flight was an hour and a half late out of LaGuardia: Air New England Flight 248, the last of the night, bound for Cape Cod. With New Bedford shut down by fog, the stopover there had been canceled. New Bedford–bound travelers had been pulled off the flight, and the plane was approaching Hyannis with the remaining eight passengers aboard. It was two and a half miles out.

A lot of things could have been different. Not that I had any control over them—it was just my lucky day. Ted Kennedy had been aboard the previous flight, or so it was later reported. The direction in which the senator had been traveling was the subject of conflicting accounts, a question that remained unanswered for me until twenty-seven years later. But I could never escape the supposition that, had he been traveling north that night, given a slight delay, he might just as easily have been traveling on my flight. The senior senator from Massachusetts: that could have made things different in a whole lot of other ways.

The plane hit the trees at 123 knots. It lost its wings as it crashed. They were sheared off, taking the fuel tanks with them, as the rest of it slammed through the forest. In an explosion of tearing sheet metal, it ripped a path through the timber, cutting through thick stands of oak and pine for a distance of three hundred feet. Whatever memories time erases, it will never erase the memory of the sound of it.

The seat belt held up. Nothing else did. I hit the belt with such force that I took the seat forward with me, ripping it right out of the fuselage. My back broke as I was thrown forward, wrapped around the restraint. The lap buckle snapped my pelvis. Through some mysterious marriage of aerodynamics and physiology, my arm broke through the steel band of my wristwatch, exploding the links—the inevitable measure, as I came to see it, of the physical forces at work, of the mechanics conspiring to kill me. The g-load peaked at around six. My forward momentum was absorbed by a collision with the upright seat back in front of me. Its impact with my face raised a welt over my eye, crushed the cartilage in my nose, and displaced one of the bones in my neck. Most of my bleeding was internal. I came to a stop with one knee on the deck, still strapped in, soaked in jet fuel.

It was going to be a long night.

The story I will tell, the story I remember, begins here, in deep woods, shrouded by impenetrable fog, in mid-June in 1979. A story of survival, of varying displays of courage attended by the ever-present fear of failing to display it, of a dark night of the soul and the days and years that followed, in the end it is a story about memory. About the things we can never forget. A story about how, even in our forgetfulness, the present is inevitably haunted by the past.

In the spring of 1979, I was half a celebrity, the author of a book, my first, that several months earlier had spent three weeks on the bestseller list in New York. I was living in Greenwich Village, I was thirty-two years old, and the topic of the book, cocaine, put me at the center of a circle of new friends and acquaintances who were far more celebrated than I.

Cocaine's elevated position in the popular culture of the 1970s is difficult to exaggerate. Periodical rights to the book, *Snowblind*, were purchased by *Rolling Stone;* an excerpt appeared in the magazine at the time the book was published. Following the book's publication, excerpts appeared in two other magazines: *High Times,* certainly an obvious choice, and *Town & Country,* probably not. Unless, of course, you were paying attention. Cocaine at the time, conspicuously pouring out of every nightclub, was no less indispensable at the hunt club. The common denominator was disposable income. To snort cocaine was to make a statement. The perforated septum was in vogue, a mark of social standing that before the seventies and coke's outright ownership of the night had been restricted largely if not exclusively to victims of congenital syphilis.

Cocaine's enhanced visibility coincided with the publication of *Snowblind,* and as the book's author, I was held at least partly responsible for the high profile the drug enjoyed. Some people behaved as if I'd invented it. But the nonfiction book featured a living protagonist, luxuriating in his own notoriety, who was quite happy to take credit for introducing the nation to cocaine's questionable pleasures. And that, along with the book's widespread critical acclaim, enabled me to enjoy my celebrity as a phenomenon with a respectable, legitimate foundation, a consequence of the same kind of honest accomplishment associated with the musicians, movie stars, and other millionaires I was routinely running out of control with.

The previous fall, with new money in my pocket, I had broken ground on a house some three hundred miles from Manhattan. Situated on the edge of a salt marsh, overlooking Cape Cod Bay, the house was now nearing completion. In more than one way, I felt I'd arrived. It wasn't that I'd never owned a house, though that was also true; it was that I'd never really had a fixed address. The eight years I'd lived in Manhattan—I was now on my third apartment—was longer by a good five years than I'd lived anywhere else in my life. My arrival on Outer Cape Cod, anchored to a thirty-year mortgage, signaled a kind of coming to light.

Having recently set up camp within the unfinished walls of the house to participate in its construction, I returned to New York in the middle of June to devote a weekend to what passed for business: the National Fashion and Boutique Show. A trade fair held three, maybe four, times a year, the show opened on June 16 at the New York Coliseum, and there I joined Zachary Swan, the former cocaine smuggler featured in *Snowblind,* who was negotiating licensing deals with manufacturers of drug paraphernalia. As a result of his efforts, a variety of products, marketed through the nation's head shops—those now-vanished fixtures of the American landscape that flourished in the Age of Aquarius—would boast, for better or worse, merchandizing tie-ins to the book.

Drug paraphernalia, of course, represented only a tiny fraction of the merchandise trafficked at the Boutique Show. But you were unlikely to see the Hallmark buyer in attendance at the *High Times* party. The party, aimed at the magazine's advertisers and crawling with the usual suspects among New York's "beautiful people"—along with drug dealers, smugglers, criminal lawyers, policy advocates, and people like me—was a special feature of the Boutique Show, a celebration hosted by the magazine's publishers whenever the fair came to town. It was at one of the larger *High Times* parties, thrown at Studio 54 (it could have been at the magazine's Christmas party), that I first met Andy Warhol. He was standing in line, waiting his turn at one of the nitrous oxide tanks. What we might have said to each other I can't remember now, and it was very much in keeping with the tone of the event that I probably couldn't remember it then. As Kinky Friedman was moved to say in such circumstances at the time, "I can't even remember the Alamo."

Swan and I had first attended the Boutique Show in the fall of the previous year, and among the first people to introduce themselves to us was a contingent of entrepreneurs from South Hadley, Massachusetts, a college town situated in the Pioneer Valley, on the east bank of the Connecticut River. They represented a variety of businesses, all of which seemed loosely associated with a head shop located there, just off the Mount Holyoke campus. A couple of them had been marketing a game they had invented, or the rules of which they had formalized, a dice game they called Cosmic Wimpout. I would meet these people again, along with some of their friends, but never really know them that well, and I never saw them after the following March, when Swan and I signed books in South Hadley after a television appearance in Boston. But I did read about them in the paper. Late on the night of June 17, two of them, along with their girlfriends, were driving back to Boston from a Cosmic Wimpout tournament in Eastham, a town on Lower Cape Cod, when a young woman walked out of the woods in Yarmouth Port and flagged them down on the Mid-Cape Highway. Drenched in aviation fuel and stained with blood, she had been walking for an hour, and she told them, "I've got to get help."

The woman's name was Suzanne, and she was one of seven other passengers with whom I'd boarded the plane that night when I left New York to return to the Cape. "A petite, brown-eyed brunette," as the local newspaper would later describe her, with straight, shoulder-length hair, dressed entirely in white, she was a nineteen-year-old college student, a Rutgers

University sophomore, and she was the only passenger to whom I had spoken at any length prior to the crash. Summering on the Cape with her family, she had been visiting friends in New Jersey, celebrating her birthday. She had planned to drive, but as a birthday gift, her parents had bought her a round-trip plane ticket. We were sitting next to each other, on opposite sides of the aisle, and when the announcement signaling our descent to Hyannis put an end to her socializing with some other students on the flight, she engaged me in conversation. She was a chatterbox, maybe she was nervous. She wanted to know what I did for a living and what kind of car I drove. She advised me to tighten my seat belt. I had been wearing it, in airline parlance, "loosely fastened about the waist" for the duration of the flight. I must have been slow to follow her advice, because I remember her reaching across the aisle and pulling it tight herself.

To a question I'm asked invariably, the question posed in first position more often than any other, the answer is that the crash came without warning. There was no time in which to be terrified or ponder the state of one's soul, to inventory the events of one's life as it passed before his or her eyes, or to calculate assets and liabilities pertaining to one's standing with God. The plane was at five thousand feet, maybe twenty-five miles southwest of Barnstable Municipal Airport in Hyannis, when the voice of the captain or maybe the first officer came over the cabin speakers with the announcement that the plane would be touching down in ten minutes; we were instructed to extinguish any cigarettes and fasten our seat belts in preparation for landing. Suzanne and I said hello, we talked for a little while, she tightened my seat belt, our conversation eventually trailed off, and we along with the other passengers retreated to the privacy of our thoughts as the aircraft descended through the final stages of the approach.

The temperature at the airport that night was sixty-seven degrees Fahrenheit, with a ten-knot breeze out of the southwest. Visibility on the ground was three quarters of a mile in fog and light drizzle, sky obscured, with an indefinite ceiling of two hundred feet. The moon was in its last quarter but lost to view in the weather. A glance to my left as we descended through the clouds revealed no more than my reflection in the window. The only evidence of forward progress was the occasional dip brought on by turbulence and the direction of the water streaking the glass. Beyond the window there was nothing but the black of an invisible night and the hypnotic drone of the turboprop engines, an insistent, monotonous hum to which I inevitably surrendered, slipping into that easeful state of interrupted animation familiar to anyone who has ever flown or been rocked to sleep in a cradle.

If, in those final ten minutes before facing potential death, I pondered anything at all, it would not have been the state of my soul but more likely the indignity of an empty stomach. I had arrived at LaGuardia before dinnertime as it is commonly observed in Manhattan. The flight was leaving out of the Marine Air Terminal—used to accommodate commuter airlines and as a general-aviation facility—and the only source of sustenance there was a poorly maintained candy machine, its age and condition suspiciously suggesting a shared provenance with the Art Deco building itself. Had I died, I would have died hungry. And tired. There is no one aboard an airplane in the hours that Hamlet in his madness calls "the very witching time of night" who isn't beat.

In the ten minutes following the landing announcement, there was no hint of what was to come. There was the somnolent drone of the engines, the beads of moisture scarifying the window glass, perhaps a slight increase in cabin pressure, and the prospect finally of home. Then impact. In the interval of a heartbeat. Lights out. You don't own it. I breathed in, fairly unmindful of any real sense of forward progress, and when I breathed out I was pulling six g's. Angling in at seven degrees, four degrees off the glide path, coming out of the sky at a rate of descent of 1,500 feet per minute, the airplane hit the trees at a velocity of 204 feet per second, breaking out of the cloud cover about two seconds from contact.

Time never had a chance to stand still.

Once the plane was down, Suzanne and I shared responsibility for making happen much of what happened, I because of my determination and the authority that attached to me by way of my age, she because she was uninjured, mobile, and utterly fearless. At thirty-two, I was more than ten years older than all but one person in the passenger cabin, and I had at least seven on him. I was a year older than the copilot, and he was out of commission. Only the pilot was older than I, and he was dead. Suzanne would ascend that night to a whole other level of hero-ics away from the site of the crash, but for now it was she and I, and what motivated me that night, more than courage or fear, was anger.

Coming around, within seconds of impact, I experienced an epiphany the violence of which remains vivid to me today. The plane had come to rest in silence. There were no ambulances, no lights or sirens, none of the scrambling you associate with an airport disaster. We had not crashed hitting the runway. No help was on its way. And in the absolute stillness of that instant, before the screaming started, I was overcome by the realization that whether I lived was up to me.

The people who operated the airline, the same people whose

indifference we had suffered for an hour and a half at LaGuardia, were responsible for this, and now they were nowhere to be found, and I remember being propelled by the resolution that I wasn't going down with *their* ship.

Raising myself up off the deck, near paralyzed below the point of my fracture, I didn't do a lot of thinking. You don't really think in those circumstances; you act, or react, or you simply shut down, control of your vital processes being the ultimate prize in that physiological face-off between adrenaline and shock. In the minute or so following impact, if I was given to thoughts of anything, they were thoughts of an airplane in Chicago, an ill-fated DC-10, American Airlines Flight 191.

That airplane, bound for Los Angeles, went down after losing one of its engines on takeoff from O'Hare International, exploding in a massive fireball a mile and a half beyond the runway, taking the lives of 273 people. One of the dead was Sheldon Wax, the managing editor of *Playboy*. I had never met Wax, but as a freelance contributor, I had worked with some of his colleagues. I had known him by reputation and remembered reading his obituary. His wife, Judith, an author, had died with him, and so too had a woman named Vicki Haider, the magazine's fiction editor.

It takes only a tenuous connection, I suppose, to see in any obituary the template of one's own, and I don't know if that explains why, but for me the crash in Chicago served as the template for all aviation disasters. Imagining planes going down, I naturally imagined that one. The crash had happened only three weeks earlier, the explosion had been captured on film, and excepting the events of September 11, 2001, it remains the single worst aviation disaster in United States history.

Struggling to my feet that night, I did, if only briefly, think of that flight in Chicago. And to the extent that I did, I was thinking of fire.

"We have to get everyone out of here."

The De Havilland DHC-6, a nineteen-passenger, twin-engine turboprop known familiarly as the Twin Otter, was one of ten owned by Boston-based Air New England, a certificated air carrier that operated a number of larger-capacity aircraft as well. The plane was fifty-two feet long with a wingspan of sixty-five feet, and there were about a thousand pounds of fuel on board when it crashed: about 145 gallons of Jet A, a commercial, kerosene-grade jet fuel, carried overhead in its wing tanks.

The silence that enveloped the aircraft in the instant after it came to rest was broken by a voice from the cockpit, by a single four-letter word from one of the crew. No urgency. No follow-up. As if he had dropped a dinner plate. Not knowing which of them was speaking, making no distinction between pilot and copilot—I knew *I* wasn't flying the plane—I thought, *Yeah, pal,* you're *upset.*

A voice in the dark. Over and out. It was the first indication of life aboard until my vision cleared. A lot happened before I heard it again. The emergency lights were dim. The cabin was obscured by what appeared to be smoke, probably the dust from all the debris, and the air was choked with fumes. I couldn't see anything or anyone beyond the forward bulkhead.

The floor was running with fuel and strewn with broken cockpit glass, and there were people everywhere. There were three girls up front, arrayed in the wreckage, behind what was left of the flight deck. The three had been traveling together. The oldest was eighteen. She was unconscious. She lay within arm's reach of the youngest, who was twelve and appeared to be dead. The third was screaming: "My sisters! My sisters!" These girls were three of the four children, one child short of the entire progeny, of a mother and father in Michigan.

The three had been seated just aft of the cockpit bulkhead, the eldest on my side of the plane. Suzanne was sitting across from me about halfway back on the starboard to right. There was one male passenger sitting behind Suzanne and another, who had been seated directly in front of her, lying on the floor.

One passenger was missing.

There had been ten people aboard the plane when it crashed, they had been thrown all over the place, and now we would all finally meet one another, those of us who were alive.

The first indication of the physical trouble I was in manifested itself immediately. The pain I experienced as I tried to stand up genuinely frightened me. In order to stand, after unbuckling, I had to simultaneously pick up the passenger at my feet, the one who had been sitting in front of Suzanne. I asked if he was OK. He said he thought he had dislocated his shoulder, but that seemed to be the extent of his injuries. He said his name was Brian. He looked to be about eighteen.

"Can you walk?" I asked him, helping him up.

He gave it a try and said, "Yeah."

The passenger who had been sitting behind Suzanne was now standing. He appeared to be uninjured but for some damage to one of his eyes. I asked him if he was a doctor. It was something I had seen him reading.

"I'm a medical student," he said.

Everything got military real fast.

"We have to get everyone out of here," I told them. "And I don't think I can carry those girls. I'm having trouble walking."

"They shouldn't be moved," argued the medical student, who told me his name was Paul.

"We have to get them off the plane," I said. "It could catch fire at any second."

Paul contended that moving the girls could make their injuries worse. Suzanne was on her feet now—her two-seat unit was collapsed on the floor—and it was she who pointed out that the extent of their injuries would mean little if they burned to death.

Evacuating the aircraft, we faced some difficult odds. We were effectively cut off from the flight deck or, more accurately, whatever was left of it, and that didn't appear to be much. If anyone up there was still alive, he wasn't offering suggestions. We didn't know yet that the pilot was dead, and it was a while before I heard from the copilot. Of the seven people alive in the passenger cabin—one of whom was the little girl—only five could walk. Of those five, I was the most seriously injured, and I operated under the assumption that, even if I managed to walk out of the wreck, I might never walk again. The pain in my back was immobilizing, I had trouble standing upright, and I was losing sensation below the point of the injury. I knew that once I stopped moving, once I was down, I was down for good; I wasn't getting up again. (In fact, it would be another two months before I was able to walk on my own.) The odds against our getting out mounted when the escape windows failed to open.

When I pulled on the emergency handles, to my mystification, they simply came off in my hands. I expected the windows to pop open. When they didn't, I hit them with all I had, and still they refused to give. It was only later, while hospitalized, that I learned from investigators for the National Transportation Safety Board that the hatches, while "moderately distorted," had not malfunctioned; the handgrips, in fact, are designed to break free, only then allowing the windows to be pushed outward. The exits had failed to open not because they weren't working properly, but because they were held shut from the outside by trees.

The fuselage, all around, was wedged in by brush and timber. An oak tree, standing where the cockpit had been, seemed to be growing inside the airplane. After the windows, the next logical route of escape was the door by which we had boarded the plane, the main cabin door on the left side. Located at the rear of the aircraft, known as an air-stair door, it was hinged to drop open from the top, deploying a stairway as it fell outward. Making no immediate sense of its operation or unable, perhaps, in the available light to read the posted instructions—maybe I feared that the windows had failed because I had somehow mishandled them—I did something completely out of character. I paused. I grabbed a passenger briefing card and followed the printed instructions for opening the door.

I don't know where I summoned the presence of mind to act in so deliberative a manner. Such forbearance is not in my nature. I'm not necessarily impatient with people, but my tolerance for uncooperative inanimate objects is low. Bumping into them by accident is sometimes sufficient to set me off. When faced with malfunctioning machinery, I am quick to lose my temper. I'm not the guy whose help you want when handling precision instruments. More than once in my life has a friend intervened, reaching out to restrain me, as my eyes narrow over some mechanical device and I start calculating the distance to the wall, with the polite admonition that I take a deep breath and "think of this as a Zen moment."

But I remember that night consciously slowing myself down and taking a methodical approach to the problem. Suzanne,

I believe, helped me out. She joined me at the door at some point. Maybe she calmed me down. I released the lock. The latch snapped open. And that door, too, was blocked. Once the mechanism was free, the door fell open just a few inches. And then I reverted to type. I remember putting my foot to it, using the only leg I could raise and groaning with every kick as whatever was behind it started to give. As soon as the opening was wide enough to squeeze people through, I quit.

What lay beyond the door was a mystery. It was absolutely black outside. It was the middle of the night, we were deep in the woods (though we didn't know that at the time), and low-lying fog took care of the rest.

"I'll go," said Suzanne—no surprise there—and she was the first to step into whatever was out there.

And that wasn't the extent of her fearlessness. Once we got people moving, Suzanne *reentered* the plane. It was she who eventually moved the injured girls from the forward end of the passenger cabin to the door at the rear of the plane. She and Brian carried the older of them; she moved the younger one by herself. The blood in which her clothing was soaked that night when she stepped out of the woods wasn't her own.

After we got everyone through the door—it was a drop of about three feet to the ground—the missing passenger showed up. He simply materialized outside the craft. This would be explained later, again by federal investigators. Apparently the young man, a Harvard student, who'd been sitting in front of Brian, had been launched through the flight deck on impact. He had exited forward, as it were. The investigators were of the opinion that he hadn't been wearing his seat belt. He ended up outside the airplane, on the ground just in front of the cockpit. Later that night at the emergency room, where he was treated and released, he was diagnosed with a broken nose and a couple of broken ribs.

He told me his name was Jon, and he proved to be very helpful. Quite cheerful under the circumstances, he had that reporting-for-duty attitude, and with Suzanne making plans to disappear, I dispatched him to the other side of the airplane to keep an eye on the copilot. Or rather, to continue to do so. The first thing he had done after getting to his feet was to extricate the copilot from the wreck.

I'd had a brief exchange with the copilot, and not a very friendly one, shortly after I'd gotten the door open, hailing him when I heard sounds of life coming from the front of the aircraft, the first I'd heard since hearing the expletive barked from that direction. Shouting in the darkness from one end of the plane to the other, I had come away from the exchange with two pieces of information. There was nothing left of the pilot, and the copilot was slipping into clinical shock. He had been bleeding badly, I now discovered. I asked Jon to go back and stay with him, and we had a quick back-and-forth about tourniquets.

I wasn't going anywhere. I was now down for good. Once I had stopped moving, it was over. The adrenaline had done its job. It had taken me as far as it was going to. My mobility was now so compromised, it was questionable whether I could even stand up. But Suzanne was another story. She was determined to go for help. I tried to talk her out of it. She said she knew where we were.

"I don't think it's a good idea," I said.

My reasoning went like this: It was not as if nobody had noticed. People might not have known where we were, but they had to know the plane was not in the air. If we stayed where we were, they'd find us.

Suzanne, however, was adamant:

"I know where we are. It's not far."

And saying good-bye, she was gone. My lieutenant had left the field.

As it turned out, we were not where she thought we were. That she found her way out of the woods at all she owed to pure luck that night, and to what I would forever believe to be (I would know her for no more than an hour) a deep reservoir of good karma. In one way, her instincts were perfect. The people charged with our rescue did not know where we were. The only clue they had to our location, beyond the designated flight path itself, was where we had dropped off military radar, the point at which the plane's electronic signature had vanished from the screen at Otis Air Force Base at the upper end of the Cape.

Our location was, in fact, quite specific. As pinpointed by one of the newspapers, published the following morning, we were "in the middle of nowhere." We were two and a half miles from the airport, half a mile off the nearest trail in an expanse of heavily wooded wilderness, 330 acres of which were owned by the Cape Cod & Islands Council of the Boy Scouts of America. Known as Camp Greenough, in operation since the 1940s, the facility, with the woodland surrounding it, featured several bodies of water, and according to the same newspaper, there were "few areas as remote and inaccessible left on the Cape." Today there are probably none. It was an hour and a half before rescuers found us. Longer still before, using brush breakers, they were able to get their equipment anywhere close. The plane had crashed around eleven o'clock. It would be close to two in the morning when firefighters carried me out of the woods.

We waited not far from the airplane, maybe fifty feet at the most, having pushed our way through the undergrowth just about as far as we could, given our collective physical condition and the fact that two of our number had to be carried. Light, however dim, emanated from the crack in the doorway through which we'd escaped the plane, acting as a point of reference until the battery powering it died. The darkness then was total. Invisible to one another, those of us lying on the left side of the airplane were spread out over an area of maybe fifteen feet square, separated by the airplane from Jon and the copilot, who lay in the woods on the other side, just below the cockpit. Jon, using the copilot's necktie, had tied off the leg that was bleeding.

The camaraderie commonly imagined when dreaming oneself into such a scenario, the noble feeling of shared sacrifice, never fully took hold. The evacuation had been accomplished in the absence of any genuine sense of it. Missing in action somewhere was that military esprit de corps. Invisible was any trace of bravado. We were draftees, a reluctant army. We had done what we had to do. Nobody was feeling heroic. Now that we were no longer channeling it into saving each other's lives, everybody had time to luxuriate in an inescapable combination of fear and thoroughgoing anger.

Attempts at lightening the mood went largely unrewarded. Shouting across the airplane to Jon to help keep up his spirits was the tail trying to wag the dog. He seemed to be doing well under the circumstances, and his good humor, as much as he tried to share it, inspired little response from the others. The middle sister did most of the talking, unable, it seemed, to stop, and I could have been a lot more sympathetic in trying to calm her down. While no doubt in shock herself, it was more out of concern for her sisters that she seemed to be so out of sorts. My insisting that she be quiet, an attempt to keep the level of panic down, was as much a sign of frustration with my own powerlessness.

The initiative was no longer ours. There had been some early strategizing, but it had ended with Suzanne's departure. We were counting on others now. Conversation was at best sporadic, as we slipped in and out of the same privacy of thought that had taken hold in the last ten minutes of the flight, those minutes that followed the landing announcement, in which all of us as passengers had trusted in a more prosaic deliverance. If the young woman hadn't been going on as she did, there wouldn't have been much more dialogue than you'd find on the page of a film script.

In the more than an hour in which we waited to be rescued, the copilot said nothing at all—nothing that was audible to anyone but Jon.

Knowing where Suzanne had come out of the woods may have helped narrow down our location. It's unclear to this day whether she emerged from the woods before rescuers arrived at the crash site. How long it took her to reach the highway is still something of a guess. When I volunteered a head count and an inventory of casualties to paramedics upon their arrival—acting as if I had things under control, with my back up against a tree—I insisted that all on the scene understand that their work in the woods wouldn't end that night until they had found the eighth passenger, the young woman who'd walked away.

What happened to Suzanne after she left me, I learned reading various newspapers. A bona fide hero and willing interview subject, she was understandably a darling of the press, and her adventures were widely reported, but only up to the point at which she finally reached help. Her declining to go to the hospital—cool with the Cosmic Wimpout guys, everything was cool with them—was indicative of what one of them later described as "how together she was."

The plane had been down for more than an hour, its whereabouts unknown to Air New England, and the airline had refused to share that fact with the people waiting at the terminal to meet it. For more than an hour, the airline had been stonewalling. Personnel at Barnstable Airport were offering various excuses for the plane's delay—that the flight had been diverted, for example—recommending that people go home and wait there to be notified. Leaving the ticket counter unmanned, spending much of their time in an office behind it in a frantic attempt to get answers themselves, they were unconvincing at best.

"I'm not going home," Suzanne's mother had told them, "until my daughter walks through that door."

My girlfriend, Mary, was among those waiting, and it was she, barging into the airline office, who confronted Air New England personnel with the understanding that the masquerade was over. In the face of their continued denial, she told them, "One of your passengers just walked in."

I spent a week in the hospital. Among the highlights of my stay was a Western Union telegram I received from my friend the Boston mystery writer Robert B. Parker, instructing me to "Recover at once." A telegram, a great hard-boiled artifact. You'd expect nothing less from Bob. We were both rising stars at the time (he, of course, would ascend to heights that not even he had the bad manners to predict), and each of us would go out of his way whenever he got a good mention to point it out to the other.

"Glad to hear you're as tough as I suspected," he wrote in a subsequent letter. "I am so tough I wouldn't have crashed."

Getting play in the press on Bob's turf was a great source of amusement for me during my rehabilitation, and I couldn't wait to confront him with one of the get-well cards I'd received.

It had been sent to me at the hospital by a stranger, a woman named Susan in Rhode Island, who wrote that she would like to meet me, and whose signature was followed by this: "age 33—blonde—hazel eyes—125 pounds—fun loving, etc."

My only contact in the hospital with the other survivors of the crash was a visit I received from the parents of the three young sisters from Michigan. They came by to thank me for what I'd done for their daughters and to return the shirt I had been wearing that night. I had placed it over one of the girls when she began shivering. I worried that I might not be worthy of their thanks. I would always wonder if carrying their children from the plane had resulted in making their injuries worse. Evacuating the girls had been done at my urging, and it proved, after all, to be unnecessary. The plane never did catch fire.

I celebrated my birthday in the hospital, I was released at the end of June, I moved into the unfinished Cape Cod house to recuperate over the summer, and twenty-seven years went by—twenty-seven years in which I never saw, spoke to, heard from, heard of, or considered reaching out to any of the people with whom I had spent that night in the woods.

On a day like today, looking southwest from the windows on the water side of the house, you can see the upper reaches of the Cape. You can trace the lazy arc of the tree line as it curves around the inner edge of the bay. Some seventeen nautical miles of uninterrupted ocean lie between here and the mouth of Barnstable Harbor—a long fetch, as the local oystermen say, an empty expanse of nothing but weather—and on a typical day anything moving this way, a vessel, a vagrant memory, is going to be running straight down the wind.

On a typical day on Cape Cod Bay, the prevailing wind blows southwest: out of the southwest, northeastward. In defiance of intuition, such a wind is said to be blowing down Cape. The Lower Cape designates the peninsula's northern stretch, its outer stretch, the forty or so miles of National Seashore hooking around to land's end. The Upper Cape lies to the south. This confusion owes its persistence to a peculiarity of maritime geography, the rules of which have been in force around here since the continent was first explored. Sailing from the inner to the outer waters of the Cape, a mariner navigates east, "down east" across the meridian lines, down the hours, minutes, and seconds of arc to a lower degree of longitude. Thus, the Lower Cape. The coast of Maine, which is farther north, is down east of here.

Life here is like life aboard ship. The marine forecast is the regional catechism. Here, weather, even more than character, is destiny. You tend to forget, on a day like today, awash in the bright blue of an undisturbed sea, that some three thousand shipwrecks lie buried in the sand below the surf that breaks along the back shore. The bones of dead sailors, lost to storms over the centuries, lie scattered beneath the shoals, strung out along the arm of the outer beach like charms on a broken bracelet.

Just east of Barnstable Harbor, which was choked by fog that disastrous night, sits the town of Dennis. A well-established Cape Cod community of some fifteen thousand residents, Dennis is one of fifteen towns on the peninsula, all of whose populations increase in the summer, in some cases by a factor of ten. Dennis stands out from its immediate neighbors, being better known to certain people off-Cape. The Outer Cape towns, out where I live, the towns of Wellfleet, Truro, and Provincetown, are home to a significant year-round population of what I like to think of as refugees: artists, writers, various entrepreneurs, escapees of all varieties. These are people, many of whom, when they dress up to go to the office, don't make their way to Boston but travel instead to New York. None of the Upper or mid-Cape towns exhibits a similar connection to Manhattan, with the exception, perhaps, of Dennis. And this is by virtue of the Cape Playhouse, the venerable summer stock theater there, which for generations has been distinguished by the caliber of Broadway talent it attracts.

Recently, I found myself at a coffee bar in Dennis. I was sitting outside, in a tiny, two-table courtyard just off the grounds of the Playhouse. I was drinking coffee and sharing a pastry with a woman who was visiting from New York. Sharing seemed to be the order of the day. We had already split a turkey sandwich at the luncheonette next door. A former retail executive, now a full-time mother of two, she lived on the Upper West Side of Manhattan, and her family owned a summerhouse in Dennis. They had owned it since she was a kid, when as a teenager she had worked as a waitress at the International House of Pancakes in Hyannis.

It was early in the afternoon, as clear and beautiful a summer day as Cape Cod could ever promise, and while dressed for the weather, she and I were probably dressed a little bit better than we might have been on a different day, were maybe just a little bit better groomed than the vacationers around us. She wore a casual skirt and a lightweight blouse; I was wearing my better jeans, clean sneakers, and a collared shirt. We had been talking for a couple of hours, since meeting earlier at the house, which was just a short walk away.

"Ted Kennedy was wearing a tuxedo," she said. "You didn't see him walk by?"

"Not that I remember."

"He walked right by us when he entered the terminal."

"So he had flown down from the Cape," I said.

"He was getting off the plane we got on."

The last time I had seen Suzanne, in the darkness of a forest at midnight, I was on the ground bleeding, unable to move, and she was walking away, disappearing in the fog. The last time I'd heard her voice was when she told me, "I'll get help."

More than twenty-seven years had passed.

When I called, I asked if she remembered me.

She said, "Of course I do."

When I asked if she would be comfortable talking about that night, the only concern she expressed was that she might not have much insight to offer.

"I was young when it happened," she said, over the phone. "And I wasn't really injured. I put it behind me pretty quickly."

Suzanne, in 1982, three years after surviving the wreck, graduated from Rutgers with a bachelor's degree in economics. Entering the buyer-training program at Bloomingdale's, she moved from Teaneck, New Jersey, and the home of her parents, Pierre and Carole Mourad, to live in New York. She worked in the clothing business for sixteen years, "always in retail, always in dresses," quitting work after a year and a half of marriage to give birth to the first of her two children. The day I called the house in Dennis, she just happened to be in town. She visited twice a year with the family, and was on the Cape for only a week. Three days later, she and I met.

"You look different," she said.

It took me a few seconds to fathom this. More than a quarter of a century had gone by, after all. What had she expected? And what an odd way to greet anyone under the best of conditions. Even under the worst of them, were I moved to say anything at all, I think I would be tempted to lie, to bow to chivalry and what I presume to be good manners, regardless of how dramatically someone had aged, and say something as time-honored and innocuous as "The years have been very good to you," or "You haven't changed at all."

Perhaps she was just uneasy, I thought. What else would serve to explain so strange a conversational gambit? Especially strange given the rather immodest belief on my part, justified or not, that I really hadn't changed much at all, or not so much as some of my contemporaries. In twenty-seven years, if only through an accident of genetics, I had managed to keep all my hair, much of which had maintained its color, and I'd gained only ten pounds or so.

And then, of course, I understood. She was not talking about the way I looked, she was talking about my *look*. Her recollection of a young man seen moving in flashes, in and out of the darkness in the flare of available light, and never seen again—an image illuminated as if by snapping strobes, if her memory of that night were anything at all like mine—was of a man with unruly, almost shoulder-length hair and a mustache that arced down to just above the edges of his chin, attributes that intensified the dark cast and severe contours of an angular face. I looked less like the typical New York author and more like an outlaw back then. The swelling above my eye and over my cheekbone that night, in evidence when she'd last seen me, had done nothing to soften my appearance. Even on a better night, you'd have taken me not for a writer but for maybe a downtown musician who hadn't eaten in a while.

That's what she'd meant. I did look different—clean-cut, better fed, and more mainstream by an applaudable margin, in addition to being older—and before I could respond, she said as much. In one way, I had the advantage of her. If I remembered her face at all from that night, my memory had been reinforced, or the image itself entirely displaced, by her photograph. Various photos of her had appeared at the time in newspapers that I'd recently reexamined. She was twenty-seven years older now—an adult version of the teenage girl in the photos, in the best of which she had been smiling—and her hair was measurably shorter. Most of the growing up she had done was visible in her eyes.

Our visit that day lasted only a couple of hours, and we passed much of the time the way people do when getting to know each other. Which proved vaguely disconcerting. For though we had spent no more than an hour together some twenty-seven years earlier, in certain ways, in ways I was unable to define, it was as though we had known each other all our lives. The time we spent together had everything and nothing in common with that which passes oftentimes in the course of a blind date. That which was most unnatural was the sense of familiarity, the ease of being together, that settled in almost at once. It was like sitting down with a stranger who knew how you took your coffee.

Looking back on the night of the crash, Suzanne solved a couple of mysteries. First there was the arrival of the tuxedoed Ted Kennedy, entering what she described as the "eerie" atmosphere of the Marine Air Terminal earlier that evening, dark and airless and virtually barren but for the plastic chairs on which we sat waiting. It was she who conjured for me the memory of that solitary candy machine. She also remembered assisting me, she said, as I worked the door through which we'd escaped the downed airplane, though her recollection of the details was unclear. In reconstructing the episode to the best of our ability, we concluded that at some point she had taken the briefing card from me, presumably to free up my hands, and had read the instructions aloud.

The persistence of inconsequential memories at the expense of memories utterly profound is a phenomenon worthy of more serious study than I'll ever be prepared to give it. To say that the mind can play tricks on you is just a polite way of saying it. Memory, in the inconstancy of its affiliations, is more than simply capricious, it's downright irresponsible; mine is characteristically irresolute, and that day when it came to revisiting events, it was as reckless as a two-year-old. As I sat there talking to Suzanne, certain significant moments danced around the edges of my recollection waiting to be invited in, while other, immaterial incidents imposed themselves with the kind of stupefying force that only trivia seem able to sustain.

One such incident presented itself as a question that continued to baffle me, a question Suzanne alone could answer, and just one more of the various mysteries I would ask her to solve that day. Why, I wanted to know, had my car been of so much interest to her? It was all I could remember of our conversation in the minutes leading up to the crash. Suzanne said she remembered the conversation, and she remembered the make of my car. Answering the question with the hint of a smile, she reminded me that her father, back then—he was now deceased— had been in the business of selling and servicing secondhand BMWs.

Seeing our conversation as the first of several, I tried to limit my questions to the night of the crash, postponing inquiry into its consequences, not only as a matter of courtesy, but also in keeping with investigative habits I'd developed as a reporter. There would be time to probe more personal issues after we'd been working at things a while longer. And so we merely skimmed the periphery, though not by name, of posttraumatic stress. Suzanne, reinvigorating the assertion that her recovery had been swift, told me that she was back on an airplane in a matter of weeks, having accepted an offer made by Air New England to help get her flying again. Accompanied by her mother and an Air New England employee, at Air New England's expense, she flew to Nantucket one morning that summer, traveling in a "small six-seater" on the scheduled flight of another carrier (probably Provincetown-Boston Airlines), stayed for lunch, and flew back to Hyannis.

I also talked to Suzanne's brother that day. Pierre, her only sibling, is two years older than she and now a professor of applied physics at the University of Washington. At the time of the crash, Pierre had been very protective of his sister, and he remained justly proud of her heroics. Without being specific, he politely contradicted the notion that she had recovered from the experience immediately, but he was quite specific in arguing against the assertion that she was largely unchanged by the incident.

"Before it happened, you were a typical narcissistic teen-ager," he said. "Afterward you were a different person, a mature, outer-directed, caring individual."

Within minutes afterward, apparently. I later talked to a lot of people who had met Suzanne that night, and not one of them recalled anything typical about her. She was deferential, not defensive, in the face of her brother's contradictions.

Suzanne was unsure how long after the crash she had shown up at the airport, and Pierre said the person best qualified to answer the question would naturally be their mother, who had been waiting for Suzanne at the terminal.

Suzanne, shaking her head, said no. "I don't think you should talk to my mother."

Her mother had been upset by my phone call, she said. The crash, understandably hard on her, was a part of the past she preferred not to dredge up.

Suzanne's mother, despite her misgivings, had been gracious that morning when I arrived at the house, and when Suzanne and I returned in the afternoon, as I picked up my car keys to leave, I went out of my way to thank Mrs. Mourad and to apol-ogize for any discomfort I'd caused.

Suzanne, by way of explanation, said to her, "I told him you don't like thinking about that night."

We were standing in the entryway of the house, Suzanne, Pierre, Mrs. Mourad, and I, and I was getting ready to step out the door.

"It was a difficult time," Mrs. Mourad admitted.

I told her I understood how she felt. It had been tough on my family, too, I said, more difficult, in many ways, for my par-ents than it had been for me. And it was a tribute to both her and her daughter, I added, that Suzanne had been able to move beyond the incident so fast.

Mrs. Mourad nodded. She had been thankful for that. She said, "The first two years were the worst."

Just like that. Like hitting an artery.

And now I have to ask myself, did I really think it wasn't there? Or was my willingness to take Suzanne at her word—"I put it behind me pretty quickly"—just a symptom of my unwillingness to ask certain questions of myself?

Such questions first occurred to me when, searching through files recently, I came across my financial records for 1979. I don't actively save such records, I just neglect to throw them out. They're stored in cardboard boxes that over the years have piled up in the basement. Stored with each year's records is a calendar or appointment book maintained on the advice of a tax accountant for the purpose of supporting my annual itemized deductions. The calendars, collectively, comprise a kind of penciled-in autobiography, an adventure story that commences just as I'm growing out of my twenties.

My appointment book for 1979 was in pretty lousy condition. It looked as if it had soaked for a while, presumably in standing water that had found its way into the basement, though the entries themselves were still legible. The fact that the ring binding was bent out of shape and the vinyl cover had somehow been slashed did not escape my notice, but failed to impress me until I began paging through the entries I'd made that year. Encountering the remains of oak leaves and pine needles trapped within the book, I suddenly understood what had happened. It had been damaged not by water but by jet fuel, hydraulic fluid, and human blood, abetted by the same violent forces that had shredded the leather briefcase in which I had been carrying it.

It must have been five or ten minutes before I came to this

realization. How could I have been so slow to conclude that the book had been with me that night on the plane? Answering that question will probably explain a discovery I find even more intriguing. The calendar entries I made in the book stop on June 16, which is certainly understandable. The plane crashed the following night. But they stop only temporarily. The entries pick up again on July 27 and continue through the end of the year.

For the next five months, I used that book, entering information daily. Itemized are visits from family and friends, an appointment with an orthopedist in Boston, dealings with carpenters and other subcontractors, progress on construction of the house. There are expenses related to my second book and a screenplay I'd contracted to write. There's a reminder to renew my passport. I returned to New York in the fall for a while. There were meetings there with my literary agent; there was an editorial conference at *Rolling Stone*. I kept an appointment with the lawyer handling my settlement. I wrote a book review for the *Washington Post*.

For five months, in its damaged condition, the appointment book sat on my desk, just one more in an assortment of necessary office supplies. Was it some kind of keepsake? A good luck charm? I doubt it. I think my consigning it to the everyday was my way of depriving it of significance. And I believe it was out of the same impulse that I put off calling Suzanne.

After deciding to make the call, I put it off day to day, week to week. I managed to put it off for over a month.

"I don't know," I told her over the phone, when she asked what it was I was looking for.

"OK," she said, seeming to understand perfectly.

And I took it to mean that she didn't know either but that she knew there was something to find.

"What seest thou else / In the dark backward and abysm of time?" is how Prospero put the question to his daughter.

Had he asked the question of Tom Waits, *The Tempest* would have been shorter.

"You can't really look in the mirror that much," is how Waits answered when I put the question to him.

We were driving around downtown Los Angeles, it was six or seven years after the crash, I was interviewing the singer-songwriter for a magazine feature I was writing, and we were managing without the blank verse. Beyond the obvious needs of the piece I was reporting, I had no reason to argue with Waits. Revisiting the past can be dangerous if you invest the meeting with anything more than a polite handshake and a "Just passing through." Lingering too long in the company of your memories, you run the risk of finding yourself stuck there.

I had resisted calling Suzanne because intuitively I knew that once I did there would probably be no turning back. Making the decision I made when I picked up the phone is more than looking in the mirror. It's like throwing yourself through the glass.

If you're going to do it, you better bring lunch.

And a stack of newspapers wouldn't hurt either.

In the dark backward of 1979, the year I was about to

revisit, there was news other than the news I was making. It was the year of the meltdown at Three Mile Island, the year of the nation's resumption of full diplomatic relations with China. Pink Floyd released *The Wall* that year, and the Federal Bureau of Prisons released John Mitchell and Patty Hearst on parole. It was the year Charlie Mingus died. Recalling the events of that year, you are struck by the passage of time—until you chance to walk past a television and stop to watch as those same events continue to play themselves out. The year began with the flight of the shah from Iran and ended with the Soviet invasion of Afghanistan. It was the year Saddam Hussein assumed control of the government in Iraq.

Of the things I remember about that year, the things I don't have to look up, none is more vivid than the speed and thoroughness with which a friend of mine managed to divert to himself all the attention I was receiving. My good friend Michael Metrinko, a former college classmate, was serving that year as a political officer at the United States Embassy in Teheran. In November, four months after my release from the hospital, revolutionaries stormed the embassy and took him and sixty-five other Americans hostage.

"I'm sure he's OK," I remember telling his mother when Mike turned up noticeably absent at the Christmastime propaganda party staged by the Iranians for the benefit of the press. I had no evidence on which to base the assertion other than my longtime friendship with Mike. I spared Mrs. Metrinko my thinking, but I was put in mind of "The Ransom of Red Chief," the O. Henry story in which a pair of hapless kidnappers, failing to collect on their demand, end up paying instead to unburden themselves of the young troublemaker they have regrettably abducted. As easy as it was for me to be cavalier, it was probably that much more a necessity, a comforting exercise in wishful thinking, and I took consolation in the certainty that Mike would have been equally irreverent had our positions been reversed.

Held for 444 days, Mike was released to a hero's welcome, and he told me over dinner one night, some time after returning home, that he found all the attention rather ridiculous: the lifetime Major League Baseball pass, the record albums, the blue jeans, the unstoppable flood of handouts pressed upon all the hostages, offers of air travel and psychiatric counseling, haircuts, groceries ... everything from vacations to vacuum cleaners.

There is nothing heroic about being a victim, he told me. "It's like being glorified for being raped."

The manner in which Mike conducted himself during the period of his captivity, a display of day-to-day heroism not revealed to the public until recently, is another matter altogether. Mike is living testimony to the rewards of a good education. One of the pleasures that helped sustain him throughout the fourteen-month ordeal he owed to his excellent command of Farsi. It allowed him to communicate with his captors more fully and intimately than otherwise, to advise the Iranians in their own language and in a variety of interesting ways, on a regular basis, to go fuck themselves. The systematic beatings he received as a result, and the endless stretch of solitary confinement, set him apart from the typical hostage, and the memory of how utterly he annoyed his tormentors will no doubt comfort him in his dotage.

But down all the years, Mike's heroism—valor legitimately exhibited, not the celebration thrust upon him by others—has never outweighed, to his way of thinking, the essential fact of his simply having been a victim. Think of courage as a fallback position. At least in one significant way, it's an expression of self-interest: You have to live with what you do for the rest of your life. In the end, to the extent that you have a chance, you don't really have a choice. There are no rewards for doing what's right, only penalties for failing to do it. That's how people in such circumstances, more often than not, end up viewing these things.

Suzanne's experience is a good example. Suzanne was celebrated for legitimate heroics, courage in the classic tradition, marching off alone in the night and sending back the cavalry. Pierre, not long after it happened, was reminded of just how deeply admired his sister was for her bravery. That summer he was driving home late one night when a police cruiser pulled up behind him. "I was clearly speeding," he recalls. Two officers stepped out of the squad car, checked his license and registration, and before dealing with the speeding infraction, asked him how Suzanne was doing. Both cops had been on duty the night of the crash and had talked to Suzanne at some point. Pierre thanked them for their show of concern and told them she was doing fine. They asked him to pass along their regards and said he should drive more carefully—"Next time you'll get a ticket"—letting him know that the reason they were not writing him up was their high opinion of his sister and their admiration for what she had done.

And still, in the light of fitting cause for esteem:

"The first two years were the worst."

I wondered how the members of my own family would answer if asked how quickly I recovered, if asked how the experience changed me. Would they see it as having made me a more "mature, outer-directed, caring individual"? For my part, I never looked at the experience as having endowed me with maturity so much as having stolen what I think of as my youth, as belated as its abandonment might have been. It took away my immortality, the sense of invincibility that maturity inevitably tempers, and with it, I think, some of my confidence, because the changes transpired overnight, rather than over time.

I find it hard to disagree with Mike. There's really no upside to severe trauma. As poetic as it might seem to think so, nothing good comes of victimization. The most you can hope for is to survive it. You don't recover, you simply recuperate. Belief in the proposition that "what doesn't kill you makes you stronger" is just another form of denial.

In getting at the truth of that night, there would be questions, I knew, without answers. The question of denial was probably one of them. Dispensing with it as unanswerable from the start, I set out to follow other, more promising avenues of investigation.

Present yourself to a statistician as somebody who is one in a million, and he'll tell you that there are thirteen hundred people in China exactly like you. Statistics, specifically the science of inferential statistics, rises out of that branch of mathematics called probability theory. Probability theory is what you get when you give God a pair of dice. A mathematical expression of the random nature of things, it has been around since the time of Pascal. In such fields as quantum mechanics, it has given birth to equations that border on the metaphysical, but long before its protocols were established, its power was appreciated instinctively by anyone who ever laid down a bet.

According to one of a variety of methods applied to coming up with a figure—the numbers are all over the place—the probability of your ever being in a plane crash is about one chance in 11 million. Statistically you would have to fly once a day for fifteen thousand years before, figuratively, the dice came up seven. If, with that in mind, you still don't like your chances, you might hope to hedge your bet by flying with someone like me. I don't know the precise odds against anyone's being in two crashes, but I know the odds are prohibitive. A friend of mine, calculating the percentages, volunteered a memorable estimate as I lay in the hospital after the crash.

"You can fly without pilots," he said.

That wisecrack, delivered while I was flat on my back, subsisting on an IV drip and 50-milligram injections of Demerol every four hours, continues to hold magic for me. It helps ease the feeling I get in my stomach whenever I board an airplane. And it remains a comforting proposition even though I know it to be delusional. Mathematicians call it the gambler's fallacy, a mistaken belief in the maturity of chances. Probability theory advances the principle that every chance event is independent of all preceding and following events. Before my crash, yes, the odds against my being in two crashes were higher than my being in one. The chances of my crashing now are exactly the same as they were before. One in 11 million.

Ask a bookie.

In U.S. plane crashes, on average—and I was surprised to discover this—nearly 96 percent of passengers survive. In even the most severe crashes, one's chances of walking (or maybe crawling) away are slightly better than fifty-fifty. Even money. Even for me. I like the one in 11 million better. The likelihood of a crash, apparently, has little to do with the fear of flying, insofar as the condition is expressed clinically. Ill disposition to air travel is as widespread as certain primeval fears, as natural as the fear of snakes, but at its deepest, as true dysphoria, an inherent fear of flying, I'm told, is a manifestation of extreme claustrophobia.

I am not claustrophobic, but I do suffer from a fear of flying.

And what I fear whenever I fly is that the airplane is going to crash. Statistics notwithstanding, I still board every flight figuring things could go either way. But board the flight nevertheless. My fear is not inherent but acquired—in June 1979—and not so much a fear as an expectation. For me, an airport is just a poorly managed casino, a joint where the people running the show don't care if you have a good time.

When I was a child, maybe five or six, I came down with some sort of infection. No one in the family can say what it was, none of them even remembers it, which leads me to believe that the affliction was fairly routine and probably of short duration, one of those bugs that kids typically pick up that run their course in maybe a week. Whatever it was, it made a lasting impression, not for its symptoms—I cannot remember experiencing any—but for its treatment, a series of shots. More than once, and it need not have been more than twice, my father, a career naval officer, stationed then at the Naval Medical Center outside Washington, took me with him to work in the morning, where a pediatrician wearing a lab coat over the uniform-of-the-day injected me with penicillin.

The high white tower of the hospital, which dominated the Maryland landscape, rising like a whale spout on a windless ocean over a sloping expanse of manicured grounds, was just a short drive from our house in Bethesda. And the first trip was no doubt a thrill, as I alone among the children in the family set off to work with my dad. The excitement gave way to trembling, of course, once my condition was diagnosed and the hypodermic needle was brandished. But the injection was not the worst of it. The shot is not what I remember. What I remember are the subsequent visits: those brief trips in the car to the hospital under the unbearable burden of inevitability, a young heart haunted not so much by a feeling of dread but worse, really, a kind of sadness, an awareness in apprehension of the follow-up shots that all my alternatives had been exhausted.

It is the same sadness I feel when I board an airplane today and feel in the twenty-four hours or so before boarding, the same heaviness that overcomes me in the anticipation of having to fly. It is a feeling, as it was during those early-morning rides to the medical center, that drains all the joy out of travel.

Like Suzanne, I was back on a plane within weeks of the crash. On a Tuesday in the middle of August, not two months after being carried out of the woods, I boarded one of the DC-3s operated by Provincetown-Boston Airlines and flew from the Outer Cape to keep an appointment with an orthopedic surgeon in Boston.

There was no easy alternative to flying. Still walking with the aid of crutches, I was not yet able to drive. I could have hopped on a bus, I suppose, an all-day proposition; I could have found some other way, if necessary. But sooner or later it was coming. There was never really any question of my not flying again. Travel had always been a significant part of my life, and it was a substantial part of my work now. How, in pursuit of a story, how else except by air, was I to get from New York to Bogotá or someplace like Beirut? And what about all that breathlessly urgent "business on the coast"? If every time I had to be in L.A. I planned to travel by train, I was facing trouble on the professional front, on that poorly fortified side of the literary life known to every poor sucker in the creative arts rather dismally as "career management." Or so I was happy to believe. Not to mention all those movie stars who couldn't live without me.

Certainly, I wouldn't be able to work right away, but I wasn't going to quit my job. Though my reputation had been established as an author and though, along with some occasional film work, I would continue to support myself writing books, like most nonfiction writers, for better or worse, I was by occupation a reporter, and it was freelance magazine journalism that provided much of my income over the time it took to complete them. Writing was only half the work. Reporting the story came first. And showing up where it was happening was only one of the more obvious requirements. I would lose some momentum after the crash, and not only in the pursuit of assignments. Writing almost anything would be hard for a while, for as difficult as it was to travel, the toughest thing to do with the injuries I had was to sit for any period of time.

Not until nine months after the crash, in March of the following year, did I resume writing magazine features. *Rolling Stone* flew me to Aspen, and for a couple of weeks around Easter, with soft powder deepening with every snowfall, I investigated a bureaucratic war being waged in the Rockies between the Drug Enforcement Administration and the local sheriff's department and didn't ski.

But my first time back on an airplane was that August flight to Boston. I don't remember it in any detail. I guess if there was anything special about it, it was my pretending that it wasn't special, pretending for the first time that there was nothing special about flying.

Pilot error is the single most common cause of fatal accidents on scheduled air transport. It accounts for over half of fatal air crashes with a known cause, and over a third of fatal crashes in total. When stipulated as the cause of a crash, pilot error falls into one of three categories: related to weather, related to mechanical failure, or related to neither. There is a high correlation between pilot error and bad weather. Such error is four times more likely when visibility is poor and a pilot is relying on instruments than in conditions where a pilot can see clearly.

The federal agency tasked with investigating U.S. air crashes is the National Transportation Safety Board. In its report, issued six months after the crash, in language immediately decipherable to aviators and bureaucrats and few others, the NTSB determined:

"The probable cause of the accident was the failure of the flight crew to recognize and react in a timely manner to the gross deviation from acceptable approach parameters, resulting in a continuation of the descent well below decision height during a precision approach without visual contact with the runway environment."

Pilot error.

"Although the Board was unable to determine conclusively the reason for the failure . . . it is believed that the degraded physiological condition of the captain seriously impaired his performance. Also, the lack of adequate crew coordination practices and procedures contributed to the first officer's failure to detect and react to the situation in a timely manner."

Pilot error waiting to happen.

To understand where things went wrong, some rudimentary information about an instrument landing system (ILS) will be helpful:

Imagine a right triangle. At its apex is the airplane. Its vertical leg (side A) represents the distance between the airplane and the ground. The ground is the base of the triangle, the horizontal leg (side B). A and B meet, by definition, at an angle of ninety degrees. Opposite that is the triangle's hypotenuse (side C), which is the distance between the airplane and the edge of the runway. Descending from the apex, the hypotenuse meets the base of the triangle—the airplane meets the runway—at a narrow angle of three degrees.

This is the three-degree glide path the pilot follows on final approach (when the plane ceases its level flight and begins its descent to the airport), riding it right to the runway threshold. There are numerous electronic components to an instrument landing system that make it possible for the pilot to do this when visibility is poor. One of them is known as a glide slope, a radio beam transmitted along the glide path from the start of the runway to the plane. Another is a series of radio beacons, also transmitted from the ground, known as the outer, middle, and inner markers, over which the airplane crosses, giving the pilot, among other things, his (horizontal) distance from the airport. To be properly fixed on the ILS, the aircraft must be at a specified altitude when it crosses a given marker.

There is an altitude restriction placed on the pilot after he crosses the outer marker, where he picks up his final approach fix and is cleared to initiate his descent. That minimum is called the decision height. When the aircraft descends to that altitude, the pilot must have the runway or its approach lights in sight—"visual contact with the runway"—to continue the approach. If not, the approach must be aborted: *No contact. Go around.*

According to the NTSB report, the plane was "405 ft below the normal glide slope altitude and 153 ft below the decision height of 293 ft when it struck the trees." A gratuitous piece of information—we can assume the aircraft would have been better off *above* the trees—if you don't understand that the plane didn't just end up there. Its altitude and descent, the safety board concluded, "were controlled in an imprecise and careless manner." So steep was its angle of descent that little could be done to save the aircraft once the problem had become clear to the copilot, the one person in a position to save it. The flight descended from decision height to impact in about six seconds, making it "extremely difficult if not impossible," in the words of the NTSB, "for the first officer to detect a deteriorating situation and react once he called decision height and verified that no approach lights were visible."

The imprecision of the approach was due in large part to pilot fatigue caused by "multiple stresses," states the report, which "in concert with [the pilot's] personal flying habits . . . and his age contributed greatly to a marked human performance degradation." Among the multiple stresses on the pilot, who was understandably exhausted, were underlying "aeromedical factors." These are itemized in the report and are crucial to an understanding of what happened. I'll get to them, and to things like "crew coordination," later.

The term "precision approach" is not a poetic construct. It speaks to the level of refinement with which an instrument landing must be performed if it is to be executed successfully. The margins are narrow and the tolerances low. The standards are sufficiently exacting that ILS instruments do not even register certain deviations beyond a selected point. The aircraft is moving fast, so small corrections must be made rapidly, but at the same time they must be—there's no better word for it—precise. Allowances for what you might call oversteering are not generous. Minor errors have a domino effect. I say minor errors because with minor adjustments they are easily correctable— easily correctable during visual flight, when a pilot can see where he's going. On instruments, he is flying blind, and minor errors don't remain minor for long.

The destiny of Flight 248 began taking shape when the plane was a few miles out, about two minutes north-northeast of the airport and a minute or so before impact, when the captain approached the outer marker three hundred feet high. Crossing the marker ten seconds later, he was two hundred and twenty feet high. He had to nose down to pick up the three-degree glide slope that would bring him into Hyannis on runway 24. Leveling off after he intersected the glide slope, he overcorrected, however. Imagine the plane bouncing off the hypotenuse. So he nosed down again.

It was now thirty seconds before impact. And he was coming in at too steep an angle. The seven degrees at which he was pitched in his attempt to pick up the beam took him below it at too high a speed. And he never knew how far below it he was. His position relative to the glide path would have appeared on the cockpit instrument panel as a full-scale deflection— the needle on his glide-slope indicator reaching the farthest point on the meter—nothing more specific than that. When the needle hit two and a half degrees, the glide-slope indicator quit measuring. Reading no deviations beyond that point is the technology's way of accepting the inevitable. Low on a precision approach by more than two and a half dots, you're no longer flying the airplane—nor even aiming it—you're just holding on.

He was angling in at seven degrees. Moving at a ground speed of 123 knots, he was shedding altitude at almost 1,500 feet per minute. As stated in the report, he intersected the glide slope in a descent "that he was unable to arrest" before hitting the canopy.

After that it was all thunderous noise and kinetic energy.

Thus ended the life of a pilot by the name of George Parmenter and the youthful innocence of several American air passengers who had invested their faith in the statistics governing such travel.

Evaluating George Parmenter's performance in the last minute of his life, a minute in which he made a tragic mistake, one runs the risk of forgetting the more than twenty-five thousand hours of flight time—more than thirty-five hundred on instruments—and forty years of aviation in which he didn't.

At eight A.M. on the morning of the crash, Doris Parmenter answered the phone at her Centerville home and handed the receiver to her husband, who just twenty hours earlier had returned from Waterville, Maine, where mechanical trouble, after a day of flying, had grounded him overnight.

As she told the editor of the *Cape Cod Times*, "I heard him say, 'OK, I'll be there. When do you need me?' I said to him, 'You're not! Let them get somebody else this time.'"

George Parmenter, almost sixty-one, a vice president and cofounder of Air New England, who flew only occasionally for the airline, only as a replacement pilot, was being called in on short notice again, summoned at the last minute to fill in for a line pilot who had phoned in sick.

In the interview she granted the editor of the *Times*, Doris Parmenter continued:

"He said a lot of people were depending on the airline to get them somewhere. And I said they never get someone else—they always call Old Faithful. And that was about the last conversation I had with him. I followed him outside and said, 'Have you got your flight bag? Have you got your notebook?' He needed his notebook because he had been working on gasoline allocations the night before—this was the time of the fuel shortage. I handed him his notebook and he got into his truck and that was the end of that."

Parmenter reported to work forty-five minutes later, scheduled for twelve and a half hours of duty. Late that same day, on the ground in Hyannis, anticipating the end of the shift, he was visibly upset, witnesses said, when informed that additional flights had been scheduled and his workday had been extended. To his original flight schedule, which called for twelve trips among four destinations, two more flights of two legs each had been added.

Parmenter and the plane's first officer put in fourteen hours of duty that day, including nine hours and sixteen minutes of flying. Parmenter's only intake of food during that time, according to the NTSB, was a Danish pastry with his coffee in the late afternoon. After fifteen takeoffs and fourteen landings, they were executing their fifteenth approach for landing when Parmenter crashed the plane.

"A prominent figure in New England aviation," in the words of the *Boston Globe*, Parmenter was a legend among local flyers, a pioneer of commercial air service on Cape Cod. Having settled on the Cape after the Second World War, during which he had flown for the Marine Corps, he and Doris, a Dennis native, founded the Cape & Islands Flight Service, which they operated for some twenty years, until the merger in 1970 that gave birth to Air New England.

"George Parmenter, throughout his airline and military career, was a hard worker," said his friend John Van Arsdale Sr., founder and president of Provincetown-Boston Airlines, who gave the eulogy at Parmenter's memorial Mass four days after the crash. "This was most clearly demonstrated this past Sunday. That day George knew there was a job to be done and he was personally ready and willing to assume more than one man's fair share."

In his eulogy, which was quoted in the *Cape Cod Times*, Van Arsdale was echoing a sentiment shared by all of Parmenter's friends, when he said, "Flying was his life."

One of Parmenter's closest friends was Delta Airlines pilot Angus Perry, a Centerville native, who died in 2003. Recently, I talked to Perry's daughter Wendy, who attended the service for Parmenter at which Van Arsdale spoke.

Wendy Boepple, now in her midfifties, is a registered nurse and mother of four. She lives with her husband, a physician, outside Boston. Wendy remembers Parmenter as "a typical Marine," and her affection for him is palpable. Beneath a gruff exterior, she says, was a man of tremendous warmth. She grew up knowing him as Uncle George, nurtured on the adventure stories that he and her father would tell.

Back in the fifties, she told me, on days when the ceiling was low, her father and Parmenter, with two planeloads of newspapers to deliver and only one plane rigged with the proper equipment, would "fly wingtip to wingtip" through the fog between Cape Cod and Nantucket. The stories the two men told, like all proper tales of derring-do, were invariably fraught with bravado: *We made it. . . . Yeah. That was easy. . . . Yeah, now all we have to figure out is how we're gonna make it back.*

Flying for the Perrys was a family affair. Many were the times in Wendy's childhood, she said, that a clear day would find her and her sisters and brother heading with their dad to the airport, where "he would borrow one of George's planes and take us up."

George Parmenter lived to fly, and to see him grounded would have been unthinkable to anyone in the local aviation community. "I cannot imagine George Parmenter as a man who for some reason was unable to fly," Van Arsdale said. "None of us close to aviation can understand how this accident could happen."

One of the members of that community was Dr. Grover Farrish, a Hyannis internist and a pilot himself, who served as the Federal Aviation Administration's local aviation medical examiner (AME).

Some four pages of the twenty-five-page accident report are devoted to George Parmenter's medical history. In 1963, suffering from persistent hypertensive cardiovascular disease, he was permanently removed from flight duty as a reserve officer in the Marine Corps. Predisposed to hypoglycemia and suffering from chronic high blood pressure, he was periodically denied FAA medical certificates, those required of a civilian pilot, over the course of the next five years. Not until August 1970, after a physical examination by Grover Farrish, did he receive the second-class medical certificate that again made it legal for him to fly. In 1971, after another examination by Farrish, he was issued a first-class certificate. And for the next seven and a half years, reports the NTSB, first-class certificates were "issued to the captain at 6-month intervals on the basis of physical examinations and cardiovascular evaluations performed by the same AME." On the application for his last certification, four months before the crash, Parmenter, when asked, listed no medications (his use of any would have required waivers) and stated that he had never been denied an airman's medical certificate. At the time, he had been on daily medication for over a decade for both hypertension and gout—"the AME in Hyannis denied knowledge of either drug"—and according to his autopsy had suffered a myocardial infarction, a heart attack, within the previous five years.

A U.S. Navy pathologist testified at the NTSB hearing held three months after the crash that in view of Parmenter's age and medical history, the pilot should have been found "unfit for flying duty." The board characterized the "results of repeated evaluations" by Farrish as "equivocal medically." Farrish did not answer a subpoena to testify. A few years later, Cape Cod Hospital appointed him chief of cardiology. He died in 1994.

Among his fellow Air New England pilots, Parmenter had a reputation for not always flying by the book. A majority of those interviewed told the NTSB that he had "disregarded checklists and crew coordination when they had flown with him." This is what is meant in the report by "his personal flying habits."

There is a call-and-response protocol between pilot and copilot required on all instrument landings. It consists of altitude, degree, and airspeed callouts, culminating in a "no contact/go around" exchange if the runway is not in sight. The copilot testified that on approach to Barnstable that night, he made all the required callouts except the "no contact" call and Parmenter did not acknowledge any of them. This is "the lack of crew coordination practices and procedures" mentioned in the report.

It was unlikely that the copilot, with only two months on the job, still on probation, and subject to termination without cause, would engage in corrective counseling with the number-three man in the company. He could have taken control of the airplane at any point, of course, and presumably would have if he had suspected trouble, but he had been flying all day with a superior known rarely to "acknowledge checklist items or other callouts from any first officer," according to the report, and the lack of such acknowledgment was not an indication that anything was wrong. By the time they hit decision height, "the possibility that [he] could have successfully assumed control of the aircraft [was] extremely remote." He told the board he never saw the ground before the airplane crashed.

Wendy Boepple, working at the time as a nurse in Burlington, Vermont, received news of the crash early that Monday morning, informed of the tragedy in a phone call from the emergency room at Cape Cod Hospital. It was her second wedding anniversary. She flew from Burlington to Boston on a Delta Airlines pass, a perk to which she was entitled as the daughter of a Delta pilot, and at Logan Airport made her way to the Air New England counter, only to be told that all of its flights to Hyannis were booked.

"I was very naive," she told me.

It never occurred to her, in what she views today as her "immaturity," to exert any of the leverage implicit in the purpose of her trip. Had she simply said who she was and why she was traveling, the airline undoubtedly would have accommodated her. Instead, she ended up taking a bus.

Her two-hour ride to the Cape was made surprisingly memorable by a reunion of sorts. She found herself sitting next to Eleanor Klimm, whom she had known more formally as Mrs. Klimm when the older woman was her fifth-grade teacher at Hyannis West Elementary. The two passengers, getting acquainted, or reacquainted, talked all the way to Hyannis, making the best of a journey that both had reason to wish were unnecessary. Mrs. Klimm, Wendy was saddened to learn, was suffering from cancer, and had traveled to Boston for medical treatment. When she asked why Wendy was making the trip to the Cape, Wendy explained to her fifth-grade teacher what she had not explained to anyone at the Air New England counter, which was everything she knew at the time from the call she'd received from Cape Cod Hospital: that her husband, sometime in the middle of the night, had been admitted through the hospital's emergency room. His name was Paul. He was twenty-five. He was a medical student. He'd been in a plane crash.

It was something I had seen him reading.

"I was reading the *New England Journal of Medicine*."

Paul Boepple, since I'd seen him reading that night on the plane, had lost some of his hair, and what remained of it had lost some of its color. His facial index had dropped a few points, but the sharp line of his brow and the severity of his gaze were all the visual evidence I'd have needed to pick him out of a lineup.

Sitting in my living room, wearing shorts and sandals and sipping a beer, he appeared to have lost none of the personal qualities in evidence when I'd first encountered him. He showed the same thoughtful, introspective reserve of the young medical student who during the flight had kept quietly to himself, the same seriousness of purpose that had led me, when the plane was taking off from LaGuardia, to single him out among my fellow passengers as the one grown-up onboard. In outer aspect and demeanor, he was much of what you would expect in a doctor and everything you would want in a pediatrician.

On a Sunday afternoon in June, taking a couple of hours out of a weekend visit to Wendy's mother in Centerville, he and Wendy had driven down to my place. Meeting this way proved easier for them than coordinating time in their schedules at home, and it saved me a trip to Boston, where Paul practices and teaches pediatric endocrinology at Massachusetts General Hospital and Harvard Medical School. Wendy works as an emergency room nurse at North Shore Medical Center in Lynn.

Paul had brought with him some newspaper clips and a copy of the accident report. He obviously had kept a file at some point, and it was neater and better organized than mine. Among the news clips he showed me was the wire story that the Associated Press had moved in the early morning hours right after the incident. Headlined "Air Crash Kills Pilot; Woods Slow Rescue" and datelined Yarmouth, Massachusetts, the story had been cut by Wendy's father from the *Kansas City Star*. George Parmenter had not been the only one flying that night. Angus Perry, on Monday morning, in the cockpit of a 727, had been preparing for takeoff from Little Rock, Arkansas, when someone handed him the paper, and there, buried in the twelfth paragraph of the seventeen-paragraph story, he read the name of his good friend George. Leaving the cockpit to telephone home, he returned a few minutes later with the information that his son-in-law had been aboard the plane that Parmenter had been flying.

In an exchange of correspondence before he and I talked, Paul had pointed to "some personal threads of the story that impact my perspective," conditioning his cooperation with me on knowing more about my "planned coverage of the events." After I outlined for him what I intended to do, he revealed his wife's connection to Parmenter, explaining that he was thus "sensitive to how the incident is portrayed." In none of our subsequent conversations did either he or Wendy frame the events of that night in a context that would suggest how difficult a time it must have been for them. But the simple accretion of detail they provided, in its matter-of-fact way, evoked a stark poetic sentiment: "When sorrows come, they come not single spies, / But in battalions."

Falling on the eve of the couple's wedding anniversary, the tragedy marked the end of a weekend that had found them flying from New England to New York City, where Paul's father, stricken with colon cancer, was undergoing surgery. From New York, Wendy returned to work in Burlington. Paul returned to Cape Cod. As part of his curriculum at the University of Vermont, Paul was serving an externship on the Cape, attached to a community practice in Hyannis, seeing patients and making rounds with a local primary-care physician—a program for "getting out into the real world"—between his third and fourth years of medical school. He was staying with Wendy's parents in Centerville. Wendy's mother, a nurse who worked as a clinical instructor in the Coronary Care Unit at Cape Cod Hospital, had helped him secure the position, and it was she who was scheduled to meet him at the airport.

The plane crashed on Father's Day.

Paul was admitted to the hospital after being carried out of the woods. Wendy was notified at two A.M. Information was sparse. "The guy who called didn't know anything," she said.

She was hastening to her husband's bedside when she met Mrs. Klimm on the bus, and throughout her rush to the Cape, she was unaware that there was a fatality associated with the crash he had survived. Nor had she any reason to wonder who had been flying the plane that had almost cost her husband his life.

"I didn't know George had been killed," she said.

Three days later, at St. Francis Xavier Church in Hyannis, the summer parish of the Kennedy family, she joined some five hundred people at Parmenter's memorial service.

"It was a very conflicting place to be," she told me. "I had conflicting emotions about what happened." But there was nothing equivocal about her grief. "He was my uncle."

Parmenter was cremated that day and his ashes released

from an airplane over Cape Cod Bay. As his friend Van Arsdale said in his eulogy, "A long, full day in an airplane would seem an appropriate way to end George's life."

Paul, for his part, didn't know Parmenter personally. "I knew *of* him, but I never met him," he said.

Wendy remained on the Cape for a week. Three or four days into her stay, Paul was released from the hospital. The injuries he had sustained were clearly more serious than had been apparent to me in the wake of the crash. His collision with the seat back in front of him, in addition to breaking his nose, had broken the bottom of both orbital sockets.

"It was like a two-by-four across the face," he told me.

I had taken the same two-by-four just above the eye.

A year after the crash, he would have follow-up surgery to correct the damage to his nose, but the blow-out fracture of the orbits, as the injury to the floor of the eye sockets is known, would permanently affect his sight.

"My left eye is sunken a millimeter or two, and I have some double vision."

The double vision is of minor concern, he said, limited to a very specific positioning of his eyes when lowered. Whether the condition had any practical consequence is a question he shrugs off, but the symptom would seem to have limited his choices when it came to pursuing a specialty. A surgical residency was probably not in the cards. But all that would come much later. Amid the chaos of the crash itself, dwelling on his injuries was a luxury Paul could not afford.

In the silence that enveloped the aircraft at the moment it came to a stop, Paul's faith in the natural order of things went largely unrewarded.

"I was waiting for the voice of authority," he said.

Mine was clearly insufficient to his needs.

"I was wearing clogs," he remembered. "I spent the first minute looking for my shoes."

From the time he was able to find them to the time I was able to crack the door, several minutes passed. And as soon as the door was open, Paul escaped the wreck. He was the second one through. While he was moving away from the plane, Suzanne, climbing out of the underbrush, was coming back aboard. Paul, all the activity behind him now, had the darkness to himself. He stood in the woods alone.

"Once the plane comes to rest, move toward the exit as quickly as possible. Fire and poisonous fumes can quickly fill the cabin, trapping you inside. . . . Get away from the crash site as soon as possible. It's going to become a very lethal environment. . . ."

That is the incantation. That, in abbreviated form, extracted here from the remarks of an FAA air-safety investigator, is what the professionals tell you to do. It is the industry-wide protocol, and Paul had followed the ritual precisely, without the help of anyone in authority. He had managed to save himself, honoring without error his obligation to do so. He had every reason to be satisfied with what he had accomplished.

Every reason but one.

Paul was about to solve a mystery, a puzzle that had confounded me since I'd first sat down with Suzanne. In determining who had done what that night, I was confronted with a simple arithmetic problem. Half of it he had just addressed. I had wondered why Suzanne had found herself alone at the front of the cabin once the eldest sister had been removed from the plane. Suzanne and the passenger named Brian had carried the young woman to the door. Carrying that sister off the plane would have required the work of two, and that would have left one other person, one person other than me, onboard the plane with Suzanne. Yet, Suzanne, according to what she told me, had been left to move the youngest girl on her own.

"I couldn't pick her up," she told me, that afternoon we met in Dennis, her eyes narrowing when she said it, as if signaling some kind of regret. She described kneeling on the deck in the blood, the fuel, and the broken glass, trying to get some kind of leverage. I asked her who finally helped her get the little girl to the back of the plane. She seemed saddened by the memory. Lowering her voice, she finally said, "Bob, I think I just dragged her." She said it as though sharing a confidence, as if alarmed by what she had done, as if there were something for which to apologize in risking her life for the child. Unable to lift the girl, she finally took her by the collar. "And I just dragged her to the door."

Her being left to do it alone was now explained by the fact that Paul had already escaped the cabin. But how, then, to explain, I wondered, getting the little girl off the plane? Suzanne had managed to do it, but not without some help. And I hadn't provided it. By then I was standing below the door, working it open from the outside. With Paul behind me in the woods, the first evacuee, the eldest sister, had to have been carried off by the other people onboard, some combination of Suzanne, the middle sister, and Brian. (If Suzanne had been one of them, she had reentered the plane yet again.) Jon, thrown clear of the plane, had yet to materialize. Whatever the combination, once the eldest sister was off the plane, Suzanne had wound up alone, kneeling at the front of the cabin with a twelve-year-old she couldn't lift; she'd had to drag the child to the door at the rear. So who carried the little girl out?

Well, by then the arithmetic had changed.

"It was clear," Paul continued, "that not everybody was able to get out. I thought, what if I stand here, and it doesn't blow up for a couple of minutes? I could have gotten them out in those couple of minutes."

He could not have stood there for more than a moment before coming to that realization, but sitting there in my living room, casting his thoughts back to that night, he seemed to be reliving an eternity as he told me what ultimately happened.

"I went back in," he said.

When I'd boarded the plane at LaGuardia, I'd taken the seat opposite Paul's. It was from there I'd observed him reading. I took the seat forward of that position, across the aisle from Suzanne's, after returning from the rear of the cabin, where I'd walked to light a cigarette once the plane was airborne. I'd asked Paul if he minded my smoking, and he'd been quick to answer "Yes." Not an unreasonable response, but maybe it was the way he said it. I remember thinking, *The guy's got balls.* It wasn't until twenty-eight years later, sitting there in my living room, that I realized how big they were.

Paul climbed back aboard, and by the time he did, Suzanne had dragged the youngest girl the length of the fuselage. Paul grabbed the girl by the armpits, lifted her off the deck, and with Suzanne holding her by the feet, they maneuvered her off the plane.

"We had to fold her through the half-open door," he recalled.

He stayed with her through the night, keeping an eye on her until rescuers arrived.

"I took her pulse, felt her skin temperature."

The most he was able to determine, he said, was that the twelve-year-old had a closed-head injury of some kind. The concussion had rendered her unconscious, and she remained that way through the hours that followed.

I don't know if it was because or in spite of the fact that Paul was a medical doctor, but I was unsurprised to hear him say that the events of that night had little effect on the way he looked at life. He saw himself, he said, in much the way a friend later described him: as a member of "the lucky bastards club." Had the incident changed his outlook at all, he probably wouldn't remember it, anyway. Paul graduated from medical school in the spring of 1980. In April 1981, his father succumbed to the colon cancer with which he had been hospitalized the week of the crash. It was a disease to which there was a genetic predisposition in the family. Paul was doing a pediatric residency at Duke University, and he and Wendy were expecting their first child when, shortly before his father died, Paul was diagnosed with cancer himself. Talk to him about survival and the conversation starts there.

We ended our visit that day on a light, though not entirely irrelevant, note, expressing our shared appreciation for the music of the late Warren Zevon. In describing life after the prospect of death, Paul had been moved to quote Zevon, who gave an answer as memorable as the songs he wrote to describe life in the anticipation of dying. When Zevon was asked by television's David Letterman if he knew anything more about life and death in light of the inoperable lung cancer that he knew would soon kill him, Zevon replied that if he had learned anything, it was "how much you're supposed to enjoy every sandwich."

My house is not strictly configured as such, but in orientation it is essentially backward. While the front door faces the street, pretty much everything else faces the opposite way, overlooking the salt marsh in back. The main living area, where Paul, Wendy, and I were sitting, is a single room that runs the length of the house, and the side giving onto the water is a lot more window than wall. It is natural for guests, either coming or going, to pause to take in the view and just as natural for me to point out to them various landmarks. But never in the years since I'd built the house had I thought to specify a geographical feature as far in the distance as the one I specified that day.

"Out that way, beyond the point, on the other side of the bay," I said, directing Paul's attention to the southwest, "that's Yarmouth Port right there."

We'll always have Paris.

Before he and Wendy left that day, I asked Paul a question to which I already knew the answer. I asked it because I was curious whether the answer was meaningful to him. The NTSB report, which Paul had apparently read, mentioned no one by name, with the exception of the pilot and first officer, so it was possible that Paul was unmindful of the twisted symmetry of it all. When I followed up in a subsequent phone conversation, telling Paul what I knew, the surprise he expressed seemed to be genuine. I had asked him for the name of the doctor to whose practice he had been attached when he was doing his externship on the Cape that summer, the internist whose patients he saw during office hours and with whom he made rounds at the hospital. Of course, I knew the answer was Grover Farrish.

I don't think of myself as a tough guy, but like any reasonably active guy, I had been knocked around often enough in my life that the beating I took when the plane hit added only fractionally to my experience of the world. What was entirely new was the g-load.

Go from over 140 miles an hour to 0, and if you do it over a short enough distance, you're necessarily going to pull g's. An irresistible consequence of rapid deceleration, the g-load is expressed as a multiple of the force exerted by gravity on a body at rest, and how that feels—and what it means—can be explained in far more entertaining fashion in the context of rapid *acceleration,* with which g-forces are more commonly associated.

In a five-g maneuver in a fighter jet your weight increases correspondingly. Your ten-pound head weighs fifty pounds. If you allow it to drop, you can't pick it up. When it's locked in position, you can't turn it. The strain on the neck muscles is visible. It's the same strain you see wrinkling the face of an astronaut when observing him training in a centrifuge or watching him leave the earth.

G-loading is what adds the thrill of rocketry to roller coasters. It's what pushes you back in your seat and makes it difficult to breathe. Pulling g's causes the blood to pool in the lower part of your body, and its impact grows more dramatic the longer the g-force is applied. As the blood rushes away from your brain, the physiological punishment escalates: from grayout to black-out to what aviation physiologists call g-LOC, for g-induced loss of consciousness.

(Redout is what happens when you push negative g's and the blood rushes the other way, visible as it engorges the vessels of your eyes. Both positive and negative g's can kill you, but human tolerance for negative g's is much lower. Pushing down hard from level flight, executing a steep dive, will subject one to negative g's—experienced as an approximation of weightless-ness—so rather than push forward on the control stick, a pilot will roll the aircraft and, with his cockpit facing the ground, draw back on the stick and pull positive g's instead.)

The progressive failure of my peripheral vision as the plane careered through the trees was symptomatic of grayout, my field of view rapidly narrowing until my central vision quit and everything went black. When pulling g's, because arterial pres-sure in the retina is less than that in the brain, you black out without losing consciousness. And if you think that's not excit-ing, try to imagine it against the appropriate soundtrack.

Imagine eight thousand pounds of aircraft aluminum being shoved through an industrial grinder, a whining, roaring, abso-lutely deafening noise that occupies every register, audible to people a mile away. Imagine the sound from inside the grinder, threatening never to stop until you are dead. It sounded like that.

I can hear it now.

Loss of consciousness would have been something of a blessing.

It was not until after acquainting myself with the relevant physiology that the experience really made sense to me. The seconds between impact and coming to rest were like entering another dimension, a frame of reference the contours of which

I was never able to delineate. It was an experience that I was capable of describing only as surreal.

Knowing what I know now explains the hallucinatory nature of the ordeal, new at the time and so unique to the circumstances that it resisted explanation. While I'm aware that the blow I took to the head might have required some shaking off, I am no longer confounded by the absolute certainty that I remained conscious throughout the crash. I don't know what other mechanics came into play in the moment of collision. I'll never know what there was in the explosive force of the impact that caused my wrist to break through the steel of my watchband or that might explain what happened to Suzanne, who told me that before standing up, she found it necessary to refasten her bra. These are mysteries I'll have to live with.

The g's we pulled when the plane hit, as punishing as they were, fell within survivable limits. And the angle of the plane's contact with the forest floor had a lot to do with keeping them there. Descending through the trees at angles that varied from four to twenty degrees, according to the crash report, the "aircraft impacted on 10.2° downsloping terrain." We struck the first tree about thirty feet up, destroyed almost forty trees before hitting the ground, and continued taking out timber over a distance of another one hundred feet, moving on a relatively flat trajectory, creating a wreckage path about sixty feet wide. The trees we killed acted as shock absorbers, dissipating the energy of the collision, which reduced the magnitude of the decelerative forces and extended their duration.

Which wouldn't have been much to celebrate if the plane had then caught fire.

"I thought, 'Oh my God, if it ever goes . . .'" one of the paramedics working the scene that night later told the *Cape Cod Times*.

How likely was it that the plane would ignite? The numbers governing the probability of fire in an air crash are a statistical mirage. There are contributing and mitigating factors, of course, some of which are intuitively obvious, but none of them, alone or collectively, can be relied upon to elevate scientific certainty beyond the limits of a good guess. Looking at it from various angles, and reading between the lines, I come away convinced that as often as not it's pretty much just the luck of the draw.

Weighing against ignition of the aircraft were the chemical properties of jet fuel, its flash point and flammability. A fire lieutenant on the scene that night pointed it out to reporters, and every pilot I've talked to since has pointed it out to me. Until now, I've pretended to know what they're talking about. Recently, rather than nod my head, I decided to look it up. The chemistry can be stated in a paragraph:

The flash point of a combustible liquid is the lowest temperature at which its fumes can be ignited in air by a flame. Commercial jet fuel is almost pure kerosene. Its flash point is about 120 degrees Fahrenheit, four times higher than that of avgas, or aviation gasoline, the 100-octane flight fuel used in piston-driven engines. Its higher flash point makes it safer than gasoline to transport and handle and less likely to ignite in a crash. Jet fuel, or turbine fuel, is also less flammable than gasoline. For hydrocarbon fumes to ignite, the ratio of vapor to air must fall within flammable range, a range that is specific to every volatile substance. And between the upper and lower flammability limits of jet fuel the range is relatively narrow.

That's it, in about 130 words. Science was on our side. But science alone is insufficient in predicting how these things will play out. The chemistry is merely comparative. High flash point and low flammability didn't help the passengers of Flight 191 in Chicago or the dead of Lower Manhattan two decades later.

(Whatever the other differences between jet fuel and gasoline, I can assure you of this: They don't smell different. Not to me. They didn't back then. For months after the crash, I recoiled at the smell of fuel, suppressing a disorienting physical reaction every time I pulled into a filling station.)

In reconstructing the crash in the woods that night, it's hard to know how to weigh the fact that the plane came apart upon impact. The fuel tanks of the De Havilland were destroyed along with the wings as the wings were sheared from the airframe. What was left of the tanks ended up fairly well back in the wreckage path. Were we fortunate that the tanks were cut away from the aircraft or fortunate to have survived in the face of the fact that they were compromised? There was a suffusion of fuel in the cabin. Everyone aboard was drenched in it. And so was the immediate terrain.

"The copilot was on the downhill side, lying in a puddle of aircraft fuel. I was kneeling in a good three inches of it trying to get a big-bore IV started. He had serious fractures, he was barely conscious. I probably did a ten on him."

Pete Norgeot retired from the Yarmouth Fire Department in 1982. He was on duty the night of the crash, filling in on an overtime shift, when the call came in to the station that the plane had dropped off radar. Saving the life of the copilot, the most seriously injured survivor, fell to Norgeot as the senior paramedic in the department.

Sturdy, bespectacled, sixty-six, one of those unpretentious, quietly competent men that Cape Cod produces in abundance, Norgeot has been interjecting himself between other people and disaster for almost half a century now. He worked for twenty years as a firefighter, and today he operates Northcape

Towing out of Sesuit Harbor in Dennis. If your boat breaks down or you run it aground anywhere on Cape Cod Bay, you can be pretty sure it's Norgeot you see when you see help heaving your way.

I found Pete Norgeot on a clear, calm, almost windless day in the middle of July aboard his twenty-nine-foot Seabird, which was tied up at the end of the fuel dock at Sesuit Harbor's Northside Marina. He and his grandson, Luke Berube, had just come in after pulling a boat off the Brewster flats. The air was warm, the humidity was low, the water was a postcard blue, and in the unfiltered late-morning sunlight, boats motored in and out of the harbor on an ebbing nine-foot, new-moon tide that had peaked an hour before.

We were seated in the cabin, behind the Seabird's center console, looking back across twenty-eight years.

"A fire would have been catastrophic," he told me, recalling the night of the crash.

The danger of it was ever present, he remembered, and the fear of it gripped everyone in the woods, most notably the young firefighter with "three or four inches of aircraft fuel" pooling around his bunker gear who was holding the Wheat lamp by the light of which Norgeot was working.

"The battery was low, the light was dim, and the kid was shaking so badly . . . let's say he was aware of his surroundings. . . . I'm trying to get a large-bore needle into a small vein . . ."

The dancing beam of the utility light in the unsteady grip of the nervous firefighter was Norgeot's only source of illumination.

"It was so damn foggy you couldn't see your hand in front of you," he said.

And when he said it, he meant it literally. But he must have felt that, as a cliché, the expression lacked the appropriate force—though *I* needed no reminding how foggy it was that night. Thinking about it again, he offered a more straightforward observation, hoping it would help me understand what he had been up against.

"I could not see both ends of the plane—*that's* how foggy it was."

Yeah, that'll do it, I thought.

Inserting a ten-gauge intravenous needle into the forearm of the copilot, Norgeot, issuing the standard instructions, calmed the young firefighter down. "Let's get him packaged and get him the hell out of here," he said, neither he nor the youngster being unmindful of the fact that once their patient was in "packaging"—fitted with a neck brace and strapped to a backboard—they would be going out with him.

Why the airplane didn't ignite will forever be open to speculation. Firemen and pilots point to the chemistry of fuel because it is what they know. What none of us knows is the rest of it. Call it luck, karma, predestination. Call it the irresistibility of grace. Experience tells me that you cannot discount the possibility that the coin will just come up heads. Two and a half weeks before the crash in Hyannis, an identical airplane, a Down East Airlines De Havilland Twin Otter, crashed in Rockland, Maine. It didn't burn either. Same airplane, pretty much the same circumstances. There were eighteen passengers aboard when it crashed, and seventeen of them were killed.

The victims of the Rockland crash died of impact trauma. Instantly. They hit the trees at eighty-five knots, which was below the speed at which we hit by about fifty miles per hour, but the distance they traveled before coming to a stop was only sixteen feet. As noted in the government crash report, the aircraft fuselage came to rest in a near-vertical position. It is estimated that the passengers pulled forty g's for two tenths of a second. "Impact velocity changes of this magnitude," to quote the report, "are marginally survivable."

G-forces were of little consequence to the one survivor of the Hyannis crash whose velocity didn't change right away. The passenger Jon, who was ejected from the aircraft, likened the experience to that of a bodysurfer coming up after catching a wave and "getting tumbled around" by another. It was the second thing to which he compared it, telling me first, when I reached him by phone in Alaska, "It was exactly the same feeling as when you're back to pass and you get hit from behind by a linebacker you didn't see coming."

At the time of the crash Jonathan Ealy, today the chief operating officer of an environmental and engineering company in Anchorage, had just completed his first year at Harvard, where he was quarterback of the freshman football team. A Los Angeles native, he had been recruited out of the International School of Brussels, where his father was an executive with ITT, the American telecommunications conglomerate whose holdings included, among other things, the company that had published my book. He was traveling to the Cape from Belgium to visit his Harvard roommate, a wide receiver with whom he had been recruited out of high school and whose family owned a house in Osterville. In the crash, in addition to cracking a bone in his nose, he "busted a couple of small floater ribs."

"I was a quarterback for just a year," he told me. "The crash and the fact that I was small and slow and not all that great kind of cut into that career. I would have been a fourth stringer warming up on the sidelines with the varsity, and the crash kind of helped me make up my mind."

That he survived the crash with no serious injuries, especially surviving the way he did, defies an explanation, but that didn't stop the NTSB's investigators from offering him one:

"The theory they came up with is that the fuselage actually expands when it hits . . . and what happened is the thing went onto its belly and sort of flopped open, and when it whacked into the tree it closed back up again. . . . What they told me— and of course I was nineteen and they were telling me whatever I wanted to hear—they told me if I spent my whole life playing pool I couldn't have made that shot."

He said that "being a very slow football player," he liked to tell his friends: "It was the only time I ever hit a hole on time in my life."

He tumbled across the ground, rolled into a tree trunk— "That's where I broke my ribs and my nose"—and came to his feet with twigs embedded in his flesh, "sticking out of the palms of my hands and out of my shoulders. The biggest one was just a little bit thinner around than a pencil, right in the palm of my hand." He figured he must have picked it up trying to break his fall. "I'd never seen anything like it. I had to pull them out, and it really hurt a lot at the end of the evening. More than the broken ribs."

Up all night drinking the night before, with the help of friends in Brussels, Jon had remained awake on the flight from Europe, warding off sleep in the belief that doing so would counteract the effects of jet lag. He had been turned around in his seat talking to Brian, trying to stay awake, when the plane crashed. It was why he hadn't been wearing his seat belt.

Facing away from the plane when it came to rest, he stood up "railing," he said, shouting at no one in particular: "How could you do this, I'm so tired!"

He then turned to face the aircraft. "I was by myself, outside the plane . . . it was so misty, and for some reason, I thought we were in a swamp." He saw the copilot draped through an opening in the side of the cockpit and rushed to get him out.

"He was sort of helping me, but his leg was completely shattered. I was pulling him by the shoulders." He was able to extricate the copilot from the wreck but was unable to move him far from the plane. "He was a huge guy, and I was really afraid to move him. Every time I moved him, it hurt him, and hurt him worse, and after a while he just started going into shock. He was in really bad shape."

Jon would spend the next hour and a half attending to the critically injured crewman, leaving him for only a few minutes at a time—in the first instance, to check on the rest of us.

"You told me to go back over and help him," he said, reminding me that it was then that he and I talked about tying off the copilot's leg. "The first thing I did was think about a tourniquet, and I used his necktie."

Jon, after that, reentered the plane twice at the copilot's request, initially searching for a first-aid kit, which he was unable to find in the wreckage. "The lights were still on . . . I walked up the aisle, and there's stuff, everyone's personal stuff, strewn all over the place. I remember a tennis racket, in particular, hanging out of an overhead . . . This is really weird, I'm alone on this crashed airplane with everyone's stuff. . . ."

The second time Jon climbed back aboard the airplane it was dark.

"He was hurt, and it was a long time for him to be hurt," he said of the copilot, "and when the lights went out, he really kind of freaked out, and that's when he sent me back in. He said, 'Get the flashlight.' I mean, the flashlight isn't going to do anything, we're not going anywhere. . . . He couldn't get it out of his head. I went back in and that's when it was pitch-black in that plane."

Not being able to see anything, which was eerie enough, was made that much more frightening by what he had seen on his previous visit: "There seemed to be fifteen miles of exposed wires," he told me, "things that looked like they could short out and cause a spark. . . . That's the part that scared the crap out of me. . . . I don't know about you guys, but I was covered in fuel. . . . That's when I started thinking, I should really try to move this guy."

Jon, administering to the copilot, was in more immediate danger than the rest of us.

"You were up a little rise and away from the plane," he remembered, "and I kept thinking you guys would probably be OK where you were if a fire started. I was literally three feet from the plane. Every time I tried to move him, first off it hurt him like hell and second off I was afraid I was going to . . . I had no idea whether I was doing the right thing or the wrong thing with the tourniquet. . . ."

The copilot's injuries were life-threatening and Jon feared that moving him might kill him, so three feet from the plane is where he remained until Pete Norgeot arrived.

A very good friend of mine, when she and I were first get-ting to know each other, asked me one afternoon over coffee if any of my siblings were girls. Perhaps it was the way she phrased the question, perhaps I just got tongue-tied, prob-ably it was a combination of both, but halfway through my response, the answer achieved a kind of immortality.

"My sister," I replied, ". . . is a girl."

My friend and I still get a laugh out of it.

I have two sisters, and both of them are girls. Elaine is the eldest and Terry the youngest of the five children in the fam-ily. Elaine was the girl who, when she was fourteen and I was eleven, taught me how to dance. Terry was the girl who, while keeping me company the week after I was released from the hos-pital that summer, taught me how to walk. I have two brothers, Mike and Bill, both of them younger than I.

Of the five of us, only Terry and I, who were born fourteen years apart, were born in the same state. Until my last year of college, we were all property of the U.S. Navy. My father, who enlisted out of high school and served as a hospital corpsman during the Second World War, retired as a captain the year I turned twenty-one. He served thirty-two years in the navy, and we kids put in varying portions of his time in service with him. Elaine and I carried military ID cards straight through to our adulthood. And in all those years that we spent in the navy, the longest we lived in any one house was maybe three of them.

Elaine sees our military upbringing as laying the groundwork for my immediate response to the crash, my apparent disinclination to grant it any significance. Two weeks after I spoke to Paul Boepple, a man similarly disinclined, a survivor content to describe himself as just one more "lucky bastard," I sat down with my sisters to talk about it. That we had never talked about it before, neither in its direct aftermath nor in the succeeding twenty-eight years, had not struck me as unusual until then, and is probably best explained by the conversation itself, which took place on a Sunday, outside Boston, in the backyard of the house Elaine has occupied since five years before the accident happened.

According to Elaine, our being uprooted with every tour of duty resulted in a certain kind of dexterity. "We were so used to stopping one thing and starting another," she said, and the pattern was established so early in our lives that we developed "skill at letting things go." Military kids, in all the services, tend to be like that, she said. What they all share is measurable by its absence.

"We don't have continuity."

Or we don't experience continuity the way other people do. For children in the habit of "letting things go and moving on," argues Elaine, the burden of continuity is inevitably displaced. "You have to carry it within yourself."

Terry, the only child in the family who spent her formative years as a civilian, was in a position to view the characteristic objectively.

"You never get used to investing that much in other people," she said.

Later in life, when romantic entanglements became complicated, others would sometimes identify this to me as being "emotionally unavailable."

We did invest in one another. The devotion and loyalty that exist among all the members of the family are as unconditional as the love that continues to unite us. Whether that has anything to do with being a military family is open to question.

"You don't depend on the friendships that sustain others," Terry said.

But it's not as though, growing up, such kids are incapable of close friendships. According to Elaine, we form very close bonds: "We form close bonds and we break them."

Contending that "military kids don't carry baggage," Elaine was referring to the virtual sort, but what she said is also true in a literal sense. Not until I grew up and lived on my own did I possess much of what might be described as a tangible or material heritage: There was never a lot of memorabilia. We as a family never held on to the kinds of things that other people typically keep in an attic. All but the essentials got thrown out in anticipation of the next move. And so the lack of continuity in our childhood was intensified by a missing history, certainly a history of the kind that you could physically sift through. The house I was building when the plane crashed was emblematic of a constancy I'd never enjoyed.

The boxes and the random assortment of old property that have piled up in the basement of the house may be viewed, by those who look for meaning in such things, as a response to my vagabond upbringing, but I think what is more telling is that I never know what's down there until I run across it by accident. Try as I might to hold on to the past—and there are those who find me quite sentimental—the evidence that I ever enjoyed one is not something I could lay hands on in a hurry. My failure to incorporate history into my everyday comings and goings has proved sweeping. My haphazard collecting of memories gives the appearance of being nothing more than some service I render my biographers.

So as not to appear entirely shameless in offering what I believe to be an excellent example of this, let me explain how the book business works, or tries to, at its best.

A first author, by tradition—a custom in force when I started out and, I think, still respected today—is seldom slammed by critics. He is reviewed favorably, or he is ignored. Book-review editors, when dealing with beginners, tend to proceed on the advice of their mothers, the etiquette endlessly drummed into them when they were children: "If you can't say something nice about someone, don't say anything at all." As a consequence, first authors in large part are insulated against bad reviews, and I unquestionably was one of them. The poor reviews *Snowblind* received were few. That they were published at all was probably explained by the outpouring of positive attention showered on the book, which was nothing short of phenomenal.

There is no writer alive who would not have wanted to be me then. The book was embraced critically by publications and people I'd admired for years. In great number. The press the book received, the reviews, the letters and tributes from distinguished authors I'd never met, were enough to fill several boxes. Mary, for my birthday that year, bought me an expensive leather portfolio in which to organize and display all the material. And that portfolio today is where it has always been— stashed, unutilized, in one of those boxes, none of which I'd be able to locate in a pinch.

Memorabilia? I've been all over the world, I've made hundreds of friends, and I've bought maybe three rolls of film in my life. The clippings I collected after the plane crash are still stashed in a blue plastic bag labeled PATIENTS BELONGINGS. Incorporate the past? I can't even file it.

Patricia—I call her my girlfriend, but that doesn't really explain it . . . I like to tell people we're dating, but she's been living here for fourteen years—Pat likes to say, "Time is a river." And in all the years she's been saying it, I've never really given much thought to its meaning. Doing so of late, I wondered who said it first. It's attributed to Marcus Aurelius—*Meditations,* book 4—and the great Roman emperor and stoic philosopher wasn't kidding when he added, "and strong is its current."

In the immediate aftermath of the crash, my neglecting to grant it any significance, at least on a conscious level, came as no surprise to my brothers and sisters. My readiness to get up and move on was a characteristic we all had in common. Able to jettison by necessity, however reluctantly, the things and the people we loved, we became that much more readily able to throw overboard the things that threatened to drag us down, things like painful experiences and memories. Dumping them was as natural in its own way as offloading those things that merely *slowed* us down: the scrapbooks, photos, and unsaved treasures that offered uninterrupted connection to our past. Putting the past behind, developing an ability to distance ourselves from the things that didn't love us back, was a necessary survival mechanism when the five of us were kids. And proficiency came swift—proficiency and speed. After a while, it was as quick as cutting an anchor line.

Having said that, however, and embracing it, I confess that I trust it only as part of a somewhat more complicated story. Not that I don't believe it. I believe all of it to be true, but I also believe it to be incomplete. For it fails to take into account the price one pays for being so squared away. In the offloading of so much cargo, by accident or simply by incident, certain provisions may go over the side, along with some necessary equipment, including some fathoming gear, any number of instruments you might use to detect what lies beneath the surface.

The best piece of evidence I have for this comes to me by way of another friend. And like the friend I was getting to know over coffee that day, and like my sisters, she is also a girl.

The day Gael Humphrey walked in the door, I was still walking on crutches. She showed up at my house the summer of the crash with a group of people down from South Hadley. She had just started work in a waterbed store, another enterprise associated with the head shop there, and she arrived on the Cape with her boss, a fellow I knew named Michael, one of the many people I'd met on my brief visit to Western Massachusetts with Zachary Swan the previous March. Swan was on the Cape for a few days. He and I would sign books at a Provincetown shop opened recently by a merchant with ties to the group, some of whom would be staying at my place, and as part of the shenanigans scheduled for the weekend, Michael and Gael would assemble a waterbed that Michael had insisted I try.

Don't take the mention of a book signing as an indication of my going back to work. It was scheduled to take place at a head shop, and it had less to do with selling books than with the merchandising possibilities that Swan had been exploiting at the Boutique Show six weeks before, which is when the event had been planned. It was more a dope thing than a book thing, more social than business, as much as anything an excuse for a party, and having recently been released from the hospital, I was in the mood for one.

Waterbeds were in vogue in certain circles at the time—

maybe they still are—and waterbed salesmen promoted their trade as a branch of specialized medicine only slightly less rigorous than that which is practiced by orthopedic surgeons. The bed, in Michael's diagnosis, was crucial to the health of my injured back, and so convinced would I be of its benefits, he believed, that in time I would agree to buy it.

Apart from a faint air of perpetual amusement that suggested she was not really a part of the crowd, little about Gael, at least at first, proved in any way conspicuous. With long brown hair and pale eyes the blue gray of cigarette smoke, she was three inches taller than I, was almost fourteen years younger, and she had a voice so soft you could sleep in it. Sophisticated beyond her years, charming in a way that radiated from the absence of any attempt to be glamorous, she possessed a rarified sense of the droll, a kind of goofball sense of humor that I would notice only later. It was not until early the next morning that I paid much attention to her. Michael by then had made his move, which served to explain all his urgency in getting the waterbed assembled.

"Setting up the bed in the middle of a party" did seem rather strange, Gael would later observe, adding, "In my experience, it was something you did at the customer's convenience."

In this case, it was done at Michael's convenience, or so his behavior suggested, and it gave the appearance of an ulterior motive in his bringing Gael with him to the Cape. Getting it done freed up my bed, yielding a double mattress, which Michael had then hauled down to the living room for him and Gael to share.

Well, she had to sleep somewhere.

Swan was the first to rise that morning, and no sooner was he up and around than I heard him talking to Gael from the stairway outside my room.

"Aren't you warm?" he said.

I stepped out onto the balcony that overlooks the living room and saw Gael on the floor below, wrapped in a sleeping bag, fully clothed, crouched on her half of the mattress, putting as much distance as possible between her and the slumbering Michael. With Swan, and now me, smiling down on her, Gael could only laugh at her predicament.

It was hard to know what Gael had been thinking when she'd shown up the day before. She had only recently met the people she was traveling with, she had just that day met me, and she had no reason not to assume that they and I were friends. They were staying at my house, after all. The truth was that I knew them only slightly better than I knew her. If I had met Michael more than once, it had been no more than twice and for no more than a few minutes each time. I was slightly better acquainted with some of the others in the entourage, a couple of whom would later become friends, but the only one on the premises that weekend with what might be thought of as an all-access backstage pass was the man known as Zachary Swan.

Zachary Swan wasn't his real name. It was the name I'd given him to protect his identity in the pages of *Snowblind*, the name by which he was known to many people who'd met him after the book was published, which included most of the people on hand. His real name was Charles Forsman, and with the commercial success of the book and the business relationship that necessarily followed, he and I had become friends. He was twenty years older than I, which made him thirty-four years older than Gael, and notwithstanding the impropriety that had made him notorious in middle age—he'd become a smuggler in his forties—he was rather conservative by nature. Chuck Forsman was a gentleman of the old school. His treatment of me, if not publicly apparent, had always been somewhat avuncular and later increasingly protective. When he died of pancreatic cancer in 1994, I found myself in a position to reciprocate that treatment, honoring a contractual relationship with the wife and young children he left behind. Given the circumstances that spawned it, nothing about our friendship was typical. You would not naturally throw the pair of us together, and the friendship seemed no less eccentric to us than it did to most other people. Ours was a strange fraternity. We belonged to a fellowship of two, and the morning we found her bundled up on the floor, the privileges of membership were extended to Gael.

"You and Chuck took me under your collective wing," she later recalled, reminding me that the silliness of her situation is what brought the three of us together. "It was a joke we shared. I didn't know how bizarre it was until I saw it through your eyes."

Escalating over the years, from camaraderie through intimacy to what might be seen as a kind of psychic attachment, the bond that Gael and I forged that weekend is a bond that prevails today. Surviving the distance that separates us and the decades over the course of which we have shared our lives with others, it is a friendship that has always been special for its silences, for the mysteries we never tried to solve. Our silences were rich, and though the memory of them today is as persistent as any I have of her, nothing is quite so memorable as the way she had of breaking them. She was a friend I could always count on to tell me what was on my mind. And I never questioned the source of her magic.

Ten years after the crash—by which time I had boarded flights to London and Paris, to Singapore, Bangkok, and Hong Kong, and other ports of call—I was writing a book on the U.S. Marshals, an adventure that, among other things, would find me in the course of my research at a training base in Louisiana rappelling from a combat helicopter hovering ninety feet in the air. With interviews for the book taking me to California, I met Gael in Santa Barbara, about two hours down the coast from where she had been living since leaving the Pioneer Valley. Bonnie Raitt was appearing in concert there, Gael had a pair of tickets, and I'd arranged to fly in and attend the performance with her before keeping appointments I'd scheduled in Los Angeles.

It had been more than six years since we'd seen each other. Gael's first marriage had just ended. Under the strain of the divorce, she'd lost some weight. Our delight at seeing each other after so much time was tempered by the sadness she was doing her best to hide, and it failed to alleviate in any significant way a different kind of pain that I had carried with me from the East Coast. Concentrated in my upper back, the pain didn't affect my gait, but when I stepped out of the airport I was in sufficient physical trouble that it was noticeable to Gael, and she took it upon herself to help me with my luggage.

The people of Santa Barbara don't need to hear it from me, but theirs is undeniably one of California's more seductive cities. Rising behind the tile roofs and palm-shaded lawns, the Santa Ynez Mountains sweep up from the Pacific over a picturesque blend of California bungalow and mission revival architecture. Its distinctive style, its geography, and its fair, forgiving weather give the place a kind of unmatchable, almost Mediterranean air. But my brief visit to Santa Barbara will always be memorable to me not for the beauty of the city itself but for the hours I spent with Gael and for a short conversation she and I had as we walked its beachfront boulevards.

Gael, concerned about the pain I was in, asked what had brought it about. I explained that it was symptomatic of travel.

Whenever I carried luggage and hauled it over any distance, I was asking for a day or so of serious discomfort, a consequence of the injuries I'd sustained in the crash. The more serious pain radiated down from my neck, and at its worst was just short of debilitating. It was far worse than the pain afflicting my lower back, the site of the more serious fracture. Arising from degenerative arthritic changes, as doctors had explained it to me, the periodic inflammation was a predictable follow-up to such injuries when the damaged area was aggravated. Occasional pain was something they had told me to expect. It happened whenever I traveled, and it was something I'd learned to live with.

"How long has it been that way?" Gael asked.

"Forever. Since the summer I met you."

I don't know if she said anything right away. It's possible she just listened. We might have talked about something else; maybe we just walked in silence. But at some point while we were walking, Gael came up with a question that, in the ten years since that summer, I'd never asked myself.

She said, "Does it happen when you take the train?"

I can try to reconstruct for you the rest of the conversation, but I'd really only be guessing. What else she said I can't remember, and what I said wouldn't matter. What I remember is her asking me that.

And after she did, it never happened again.

I called to remind her of it recently, and I could hear her smiling over the phone. That she is always smiling about something is part of Gael's enchantment. That her smile is actually audible is one of the spells she's cast on me. She declined to take more than half the credit for relieving me of the affliction. I'd identified the encumbrance on my own, she said. She had merely identified the brand.

"It was a different kind of baggage you were carrying."

I've come to see the affliction as what happens when muscle memory breaks bad.

In the church of practice-makes-perfect, no principle is more sacred, no icon before which they genuflect more worthy of glorification, than what instructors call muscle memory. You hear it from them all the time. It's an expression I associate through personal experience with endeavors like small-arms training and learning to play the piano. Neuromuscular memory develops over time, through repetition of a sequence of motor skills until their coordination is automatic. Commonly referred to as muscle memory, it will save your life in a gunfight and lead your fingers through "Harlem Nocturne" without your having to think. It's what enables you to tie your shoes. Muscle memory is what people are talking about when they tell you, "It's just like riding a bike."

In any neuromotor process, your brain is exchanging information with the parts of your body that move. In the exercise of muscle memory, your mind and your body are reminiscing. My back pain reflected a conversation I'd never openly had with my injuries, a memory my mind and my body were sharing below the threshold of my awareness. Maybe it was the sound of landing gear or the whine of a turbine engine, maybe it was the smell of an airport; it could have been the orchestration of a variety of sensory cues, but whatever provoked the dialogue, my subconscious was telling my back muscles, "Hey, they're playing our song." And everything tightened up.

I might have forgotten the words, but my body remembered the music.

As skilled as I was at letting things go—"and moving on," as suggested by my sister Elaine—as successful as I had been, or thought I had been, at putting the crash out of my mind, it lay there beneath the surface. And like the fingering of some Beethoven piece long left unrehearsed, my body remembered it for me, a realization to which Gael directed me ten years after the fact. And she did it with a simple question. I don't know where I lost the means necessary to realize it on my own, or even if I ever possessed the means, but once I was introduced to the source of my suffering, I ceased to be its victim. I concede this with some misgiving, for I fear it can only further encourage those who dwell among us who persist in the practice of psychoanalysis. The source of my salvation lay elsewhere. I see it in the heavenly witchcraft of a friend I never stopped loving and whose magic has never failed me.

S uzanne walked out of the woods sometime after midnight on the eastbound side of the Mid-Cape Highway. Jim Bernier, by then, was celebrating the end of a day that even by the standards of the time he could honestly describe as "ridiculously excessive." Bernier, twenty-eight, and his girlfriend, Kammy Tribus, along with their friends Terry Opperman and Debbie Oster, had been part of a gathering of between "a hundred and two hundred" people who had convened on the Lower Cape for a Cosmic Wimpout tournament twelve hours earlier, though the taking of refreshments had begun before that.

"Everybody had been partying all day long," Bernier says.

Bernier was already known to many of those who had made the pilgrimage to Eastham, being one of the few people on what could be considered the Cosmic Wimpout payroll. Fulfilling mail orders out of the South Hadley head shop where Cosmic Wimpout was based, he was the familiar interface between the game and its legion of players throughout the country. The only other person as closely associated with the game was Bernier's friend Jim Rice, also known as Maverick, the young lawyer who had introduced himself to me at the Boutique Show the previous fall. Rice, who also attended the Eastham tournament, was recently described to me as the dice game's "founding father."

"While I did (with some others) bring the game to the valley,"

Rice modestly concedes, "at the time, I was just another clown, just another member of the Amorphous Cosmic Wimpout Traveling Circus."

Bernier and his companions, in Opperman's pale yellow Chevy Impala, left the gathering in Eastham and headed for Boston, about eighty-five miles away. Opperman was driving, Oster was sitting up front with him, and Bernier and Tribus were reclining in the rear seat of the "well-seasoned" sedan. They were about twenty miles into the trip, west of the highway exit for Yarmouth, when Suzanne stepped out of the woods into the glare of the Chevy's headlights.

None of the four, Bernier says, harbored illusions about what was coming. What they saw was certainly odd, but nothing about it was funny.

"Whoa, this is not good," went the collective thinking inside the car.

Bernier today works as a legal assistant in a Cambridge, Massachusetts, law firm with which Rice's practice shares offices. I caught up with him on a Sunday morning at the Boston apartment just off Commonwealth Avenue that Rice has occupied since his days as a Boston University student. It was two days before Christmas. The streets of the city were covered with snow. Rice was out of town for the holidays. The third-floor apartment, a spacious remnant of former student housing at BU, was artfully cluttered with memorabilia dating to the seventies, having changed little, according to Bernier, since the day Rice had moved in.

Bernier served coffee, and we sat in the living room, where we talked for a couple of hours. The television was on, but the sound had been muted. Bernier, who had been watching a news program before I showed up that morning, couldn't see the TV, and I paid it no attention until midway through our conversation, when a movie came up on the screen, silent, yet unignorable, almost ridiculous in how fitting and proper it was in light of the discussion under way: the 1969 counterculture classic *Easy Rider*. A cinematic period piece in which peace, love, dope, and tragedy sentimentally converge, it appeared as if part of the set decoration, an accessory to the apartment. You couldn't have stipulated a more appropriate backdrop. Its advent brought a certain hallucinatory quality to the endeavor.

If Bernier had changed since the seventies, you wouldn't have known it from me. I had a vague memory of a bearded, soft-spoken fellow, maybe six feet tall, with shoulder-length hair. The beard was now gone, and what was left of his brown hair issued in long strands from beneath the crown of a base-ball cap to a point well below the temples of his eyeglasses. Jim Bernier was no slave to fashion. Wearing work boots, blue jeans, and more than one shirt, he fell on a sartorial scale some-where "between a lumberjack and a hippie," which is how Gael Humphrey had answered when I'd asked her to be more spe-cific in recalling the old friend whom she'd lovingly described as "unkempt."

Gael and Bernier had known each other pretty well in South Hadley. Like all his friends, she knew him as Jeb, the acronym that incorporated his middle initial. Today, she says, Jeb still holds a place among the more intelligent people she's ever known, and she recalls his having "one of the quickest wits . . . really, really funny." Bernier admits to having given people back then "the impression that I had it together more than I did." Gael remembers being saddened by what she refers to as an "unfortunate drinking problem," so he didn't give that impression to *her*, though she is quick to add that his intemper-ance never obscured a "soft and sweet heart."

I found nothing in my conversations with Bernier, who'd

been sober for more than sixteen years, to contradict what Gael said about his intelligence or his wit, or even his heart, for that matter—he is one of the more thoughtful and articulate of the people I talked to—but what struck me about him initially was his extraordinary memory.

"It rarely fails me," he admitted. "For good and for ill. There are nights, and entire presidential administrations, that I wish I could erase completely."

He has possessed it since childhood, he said.

I knew that I had met Bernier, if only briefly, at some point prior to the crash. He remembered the moment and the circumstances precisely. I was introducing myself to him and a woman friend of his, he said, when her dog—a troubled mutt who had managed to find in his owner "the only person who loved him"—jumped up and made "such a mess" of me that I had to change my clothes. I don't remember the encounter (Bernier claims I handled it well), but I do remember the day. It had to have been Saturday, March 13, the fourth day of the meltdown at Three Mile Island, the day in 1979 that Zachary Swan and I signed books in South Hadley. It's in the calendar I carried on the plane.

Equally memorable to Bernier was the moment he first saw Suzanne.

"There was unanimous and immediate recognition that she was in trouble," he told me. That she stood there alone—there was no car, no sign of a breakdown—made her appearance all the more ominous. "It looked serious, but it also looked seriously strange."

For Bernier and his friends, strange circumstances were a common occurrence, given "the way everybody was living life at the time," and by that measure, he said, "this was not so extraordinary. 'First, do no harm': That's pretty much how we were living in those days. Avoid violence and legal problems, and everything else was just fine."

As soon as Opperman saw Suzanne, standing there in the light of his headlamps, he pulled the car over.

"Terry did exactly what I expected him to do. And he didn't need any help from me or Kammy or Debbie. If Terry had reacted differently . . . I'm sure Kammy or Debbie would've told him to stop."

Bernier confessed that considering the . . . let's call it festive . . . nature of the expedition, he invited some legal risk stopping that night, knowing that he might eventually be dealing with the police. He and Opperman identified themselves to Suzanne as the Cosmic Wimpout Clowns. But none of that came into consideration. Neither for him nor any of the others. "There are certain things you do because of who you are, no matter how uncomfortable they make you."

He might just as easily have been referring to Suzanne's behavior that night.

"Given the situation she was in, it was amazing how together she was." He was not alone in that assessment. All four travelers that night were "struck by how heroic this person was."

When I asked if he'd been helpful in directing authorities to where Suzanne had exited the woods, he said, "Most of that is to the victim's credit," pointing out that Suzanne "was in shock *and* she was composed." Expressing again his admiration for how well she handled things that night, he was unequivocal in asserting, "She was a hero. Four out of five of her peers would have been useless."

Suzanne asked to be taken to the airport rather than the hospital, presumably seeing it as the more direct approach to completing her mission. In the end, her choice was the perfect choice, eliminating as it did numerous links in the chain of communication. When they arrived at the airport, Bernier waited in the car with the women, and Opperman walked Suzanne into the terminal.

And shortly thereafter the Cosmic Wimpout Clowns, having served what they saw as their purpose, were back on the road.

"At the end of what we'll politely call a full day."

The crash, reported nationally, dominated the regional news. The *Boston Globe* ran the story under a page-one banner headline. All the broadcast media led with it. My sister Elaine was driving to work that Monday morning, listening to all-news radio, picking up local weather and traffic, when the report of the crash came over the air.

And I was mentioned as one of the passengers.

"I almost went off the road," she said. "When I got to work, I couldn't breathe." So distraught was she ". . . I was crying . . . my brother, my brother . . ." that it fell to her colleagues to put in the call to my parents, who by then had received word themselves and were leaving for the hospital.

My parents, who lived outside Boston not far from Elaine, had learned of the crash from a nephew, whose daughter had caught the news that morning watching television. He phoned, got my mother, asked her, "How's Bob?" and then had to explain to her why he was calling.

The premature release of my name to the press was probably inevitable under the circumstances.

My girlfriend, Mary, with a couple of weeks off before starting a new job in New York, had joined me on the Cape to work on the house. She was waiting for me at the airport that night, and she made her way to the hospital after Suzanne walked in with news of the crash. She was there when paramedics brought me in by ambulance. A native New Yorker, the force of whose personality matched that of anyone in the building, Mary was as smart, well educated, and experienced as any of the professionals on hand. A nurse herself, who came by her skepticism honestly, she knew better than to take anybody's word for anything, and moreover, she knew how things worked. Moving unimpeded through the emergency room, no stranger to the territory—it was turf as familiar to her as were the streets of Manhattan—she told the hospital staff what they needed to hear. She told them she was my wife.

From whatever angle you viewed the disaster, or any disaster, for that matter, in looking for someone to cover your back, you'd look in vain for someone better suited to it than Mary. She had all the qualifications. It was like going into combat with a Navy SEAL on the team. In addition to being a registered nurse, she held a graduate degree in public health, she had just been hired as risk manager of a major New York hospital, and three of her brothers were lawyers. The only way things could have worked out better is if she'd known how to fly a plane.

As far as either the hospital or the airline was concerned, Mary's presence on the scene that night, identified as my wife, constituted the necessary "notification of next of kin," pending which my name was being withheld from the press. Whether my name would have been released had she said she was my girlfriend, I really don't know. The question would have been academic, had it not been the middle of the night. She was not going to call my family until she had answers, and by the time she had them, it was three in the morning. She didn't leave the hospital until four. When my parents tried to reach her at the house, she was asleep at a motel in Hyannis. But she had left word that I was OK. Having seen and talked to me, examined my chart, and debriefed the surgeons and orthopedists who were treating me—*while* they were treating me—she was able to say so with professional confidence.

By then I was out cold on narcotics.

Mary, whom I had met at a party four and a half years earlier, and with whom I had fallen hopelessly in love a couple of heart-beats thereafter, was in fact to become my wife, and eventually to become my ex-wife. We were married for the last thirteen of our twenty years together. Every marriage has its difficulties, and ours was no exception, but none compared with how difficult the marriage was to give up. When recently I traveled to New York to ask her what she remembered about the crash, it had been more than eleven years since we'd last seen each other. Nor in almost as many years, apart from my calling to arrange the visit, had we spoken to each other more than twice. Both of those conversations had taken place in 2001, the first when my father died early that year, the second in September, when I called to inquire about her brother, a federal agent who had worked out of an office at the World Trade Center in Man-hattan. (He had by that time been transferred to his service's headquarters in Washington.) Both conversations followed five years of silence and had taken place on exceptional occasions. The conversations themselves were exceptional for the fact that they were polite.

Truth is not the only daughter of Time.

Arriving at the apartment that she and I had once shared, the apartment in which I had lived alone for four years prior to our marriage, I was sensitive to every nuance, a reporter alert to every detail, only to find my efforts at observation entirely confounded. The apartment had changed more than she had, and it had changed hardly at all. Walking into an environment that held so many memories for me, seeing her after so long, I was prepared to be overwhelmed by a rush of emotions, all of which I would record, but what erupted in me most dramatically was the experience of their absence.

There was a matter-of-fact quality to our being together, a nonchalance I probably should have anticipated. One of the things I might have been more mindful of in advance of our meeting was that Mary, over the course of our twenty years together, had always been respectful of my work and tireless in her support of it. Nothing during that time saddened her more than watching me neglect it. Nothing would be more important to her now than the success of the task at hand, and nothing was more matter-of-fact than her report on the events of that night.

The passenger terminal at Barnstable Airport in 1979 was no less dehumanizing than that of any other airport, only less pretentiously so. Displaying much the same dispiriting atmosphere as the Marine Air Terminal at LaGuardia, it exhibited all the charm and none of the interesting characters of a bus station late at night.

Throughout the delay, on the night of the crash, the people waiting to meet the plane had been seeking information from Air New England's agents on the ground. Mary herself, on two occasions, had approached the ticket counter to confront the agents with questions. Something was wrong, but with airlines something was always wrong. Her first clue that something was *really* wrong, that things were going to be different this time, was "when they stopped communicating," she told me, "when they physically removed themselves."

Something had changed.

"I don't know what they knew, but they disappeared," she said.

At that point, the tension escalated. Apprehension mounted with it, and the outlines of a tragedy took shape. All the indications were there. The word "disaster," unspoken, insinuated itself into the silence until it could no longer be denied. The word was made flesh when Suzanne walked through the door.

Mary spent the first minute or so settling Suzanne's mother down. Once Mrs. Mourad had regained her composure, Mary turned her attention to Suzanne.

"They sit, I'm waiting patiently," she told me, "so I can ask the daughter something."

But she didn't ask it right away. Instead, she addressed more urgent, procedural issues, asking Suzanne the kinds of questions an emergency worker might ask, things like "How did you get here? How long has the plane been down?"

"Back and forth," as Mary described it. "I'm pacing myself. Do I really want to know the answer to the only question I want to ask . . . ?"

And finally she asked the question.

"'My boyfriend was on the plane . . .'"

And she described me to Suzanne.

" 'You mean the author . . .'"

Mary paused a second before saying yes.

". . . I'm getting closer now to the answer," she told me.

" 'He helped everybody get off.'"

And that was it, Mary told me, as far as she was concerned.

"You were off the plane," she said. "That was all I cared about."

All of this transpired before Air New England employees, locked inside their office, had been made aware of Suzanne's arrival. After hearing that I was alive, Mary banged on the office door and, ignoring their feeble protests now, told them, "There's somebody out here I think you should talk to."

Mary and I spent a little more than two hours together remembering the events of that night. I was reminded that much of who I was and who I would probably always be grew out of my years with her. If in any significant way I was now that "more mature, outer-directed, caring individual" I'd wondered about, it was not because of the crash but thanks in large part to her. Continually, before and after the crash—she and I married three years after it—she'd tried to change me for the better, succeeding in a way I proved incapable of exhibiting, sadly and probably inevitably, until we said good-bye.

We talked a while at the apartment, then walked over to Sheridan Square to a Mexican restaurant she wanted to try. We inquired after each other's families. We talked briefly about her work. We didn't talk about our personal lives. I was curious but didn't ask. I could live with knowing only as much about her as she cared to volunteer. She looked good, she seemed to be well, and she appeared to be happy. That was enough for me. She was off the plane. That was all I cared about.

She had work to do. I had a train to catch. I made my way uptown, thinking about something she said to me just before we said good night. It was a remark quite characteristic of Mary, who during our days together rarely let a minute go by without giving me something to think about. I wasn't quite sure what she meant by it. I'm not sure I was supposed to. It was one of those conversational attention-getters that had always enlivened our day-to-day discourse, a throwaway line that could be counted on to open up the intellectual terrain, a little taste of excess on the road to the palace of wisdom. Here now it came in closing, a parting gift, a conundrum I could puzzle out when in need of a little intrigue.

"Those weren't good days," she told me. "We just thought they were."

I'm still wondering: What's the difference?

While Suzanne was fighting her way out of the forest, paramedics were fighting their way in, and they had no way of knowing what they might find once they located the wreck. Said one of them, William Smith: "Plane crashes that don't have people dead on 'em are few and far between."

Dead and in the kind of condition that makes it tough for firefighters to sleep at night.

Well over an hour went by before we sensed their presence in the woods. When we did, we called out to them. And at the sound of life in the distance, their level of urgency escalated.

"We hear the screaming," Pete Norgeot recalled, "but the screams are all diffused."

In the fog, it was difficult to determine the direction from which the shouts were coming.

"We have no idea where they are," EMT Bob Jenney said of the survivors whose voices he could hear.

And then, almost two hours into the search, in the vaporous light of a utility lamp, like some half-buried Yucatán pyramid overgrown by vegetation and stumbled upon in the jungle by astonished archaeologists, there suddenly appeared, as Smith described it, rising up before them, "this great big airplane in the woods."

Smith, thirty-seven, a full-time firefighter and paramedic with four years on the job at the time, answered the call from home in Yarmouth wearing Top-Siders and a T-shirt and went into the woods that way. He was dressed only a little less casually when I met him twenty-eight years later in East-ham. Five nine, two hundred pounds, with enough red in his handlebar mustache to indicate the color from which his full head of hair had by now gone entirely gray, he answered the door wearing walking shorts and a polo shirt, as neat, well scrubbed, and shipshape as the house into which he invited me, a small, two-bedroom cottage he shared with the woman he called his life partner, Debbie Abbott, the executive assistant to the town's fire chief. Abbott was away at work when I visited.

"You'll see a house with tacky flamingos out front. That's me," Smith had said when I called. It made the place easy to find. Out front, I saw only a couple of them, but Smith would later assure me that more flamingos, about "two dozen total," occupied other parts of the small property. "Lots of plastic flamingos," he said, "made in Massachusetts."

Coffee was brewing when I arrived. The second thing Smith did was pour me a cup. The first thing he did was apologize.

"It was probably the most significant day of your life," he said, "and to me it was just another plane crash."

My crash had been the second of three to which Smith responded in his twenty-four years on the job. The others were of smaller craft, but he wasn't making a point about plane crashes. He was speaking to one of the unofficial qualifications for work as a firefighter and paramedic.

"If I saw you the next day on the street, I wouldn't know you," he said. "God took care of me there. I never remembered the patient. I never carried their faces around with me. But I recall vividly every location."

Smith and I hadn't met that night. I hadn't been his patient.

What little he did remember about his patient suggested to me that the survivor he treated had almost certainly been the middle sister.

"I carried a woman out of the woods," he said. "She appeared to be young. She was conscious." He remembered starting an IV on her, and he remembered the IV coming out. He remembered stopping for that and stopping frequently with the other stretcher-bearers, both to catch a breather and, just as important, to gain a footing. "You couldn't walk out on the path you walked in on."

Rescuers had come in behind brush breakers, climbing over fallen trees that were inclined now in the wrong direction.

According to newspaper accounts of the crash, the rescuers carried survivors a mile to waiting ambulances. "It was at least sixteen miles as far as I was concerned," Smith told the *Cape Cod Times,* in an interview published a week after the crash.

He worked the crash until six, he said, and had to be on duty that morning at eight, at which time he responded to a building fire, so it was not until later that afternoon that he and other firefighters had an opportunity to sit and reflect upon the disaster. Such reflection, a collective debriefing of sorts, was ordained by long-standing tradition.

Pete Norgeot, when he and I talked, said that while post-traumatic stress disorder might be better understood today, firefighters are "still the same morons running into a burning building while everyone else is running out." Like Smith, a paramedic lucky never to carry the faces of his patients around with him, Norgeot spoke of the "selective amnesia" that enables all firefighters to do their job, the survival mechanism that kicks in "when you realize you can't sleep." Fire-and-rescue work brings with it, he told me, "things you don't need constant reminders of." You have to be able to put those things behind you when you go home, "to be able to go back and go to sleep. You have to learn to do that or it will destroy you." Sleeping is not something that comes easy, he said, "when you see body parts all over the ceiling."

Stress counseling as we know it today wasn't available then to first responders, and the prevailing therapy for firefighters, Smith told me when I visited him that day at his cottage, was the "choir practice" we associate with cops, the getting together after the shift ends for rounds of drinking and talking.

And, when necessary, more drinking.

"Savin' lives, I did that for a livin'," and did it for the next twenty years, he told me, until he was forced out of the department.

Smith today gives the impression of a man who has put some significant distance between him and the drinking.

Before I left, I showed Smith a picture. It had run on page one below the fold of the Sunday *Cape Cod Times*, to the left of the article in which he had been quoted. It was a picture of me, on my back in the woods, and leaning over me was an unidentified fireman. This was the paramedic who had treated me, and I was hoping to track him down. His helmet visor obscured his face, and none of his uniform insignia were sufficiently distinctive to identify him, so all Smith could do was guess.

I would show it to as many veterans as I could talk to.

When the paramedic appeared over me that night, I told him how many survivors there were and said that all of us were outside the wreck. I told him there were two people on the other side of the fuselage, and one person had set off looking for help. I said I didn't know the extent of the first officer's injuries but believed them to be severe, and that the two girls lying off to my left were injured more seriously than I.

What he communicated to other firefighters, if anything, I can't remember now, but whatever he said, whether to them or to me, was sufficient to quiet me down after that, and the triage proceeded of its own momentum without further input from me.

"I'm just going to check you out," he said, and started patting me down, looking for things like broken bones and all the terrible stuff that can happen to people when they drop out of the sky without parachutes.

"Whoa, what's this?" he wanted to know, when his hands lighted upon a swelling above my ankle. "Can you feel that?"

"It's money," I told him.

He seemed relieved.

"I'm going to take it out," he said. "And I'm going to put it in your pocket, OK?"

"OK."

He hiked up my cuff, and from inside my sock, where the currency was folded, he removed the five thousand dollars I was carrying.

"I'm taking it out," he said, showing it to me. "Here it is."

"OK."

The care he took in reassuring me at every step in the transfer gave the whole endeavor the flavor of an ancient shadow play.

"I'm putting it in your pocket."

And with that he stuffed the fifty hundreds into one of the tight side pockets of my jeans.

"It's in your pocket, OK?"

"OK."

The consideration he showed was indicative of the way he treated me throughout the next few hours.

I was reminded of this moment a few days later, during one of the visits I received from the airline rep, a very nice fellow I got to know over the week I was confined to the hospital. I can't recall his title. I think he was some kind of public-affairs or customer-relations guy. Risk management was probably a part of the job description. I don't think he was a lawyer. I remember him only as tall and fair and always a pleasure to talk to. Suzanne says his name was Rick. He was the local Air New England employee who later accompanied her on her flight to Nantucket. He had shown up at the foot of my bed soon after my condition had stabilized.

To me—and I assume, to the other survivors—he was the identifiable face of the airline. He was the company front man in the matter of the crash, the one employee of the airline I would meet. I don't know where he was when the plane disappeared, but whenever I think of the people at the airport who were lying to Mary that night or of the person there who kept asking Suzanne if she was sure she hadn't crossed the highway, I envision a guy who looks like Rick. But he was a very nice guy for all that. While I was in the hospital, he visited me regularly, answering questions, passing on information, and always making sure I had everything I needed. In the crash, I had lost my eyeglasses, and I think he was the one who, once they'd been found and inventoried, delivered them to me on the ward. There was an informality to our relationship. Everything about it was casual. It couldn't have been more relaxed. It was like that of any two people doing business together who have agents overseeing the deal points. Rick and I were just friends. *That other stuff? That's up in legal.* The airline's folks at Lloyds of London, my "representatives" at 99 Park. *Somebody's handling that.*

I can't say so with certainty, but I want to say Rick was engaged. I seem to remember saying hello to a young woman who came in with him on the weekend, someone he brought by to meet me. (Suzanne believes they were married.) Not that it's particularly important. I offer it as one more illustration of the friendship we both pretended was personal.

Not that I doubted the sincerity of the kindness Rick displayed. If he was doing what he had to do, he was doing exactly what I would have done if I'd accidentally injured somebody. If thrown together under other circumstances, we might very well have become friends. He seemed to be my kind of guy. Nor was I ever suspicious of his motives. Yes, he worked for the airline, and I was careful not to volunteer anything that I thought might prejudice my damage claim and that he might feel obliged to share with his employers, but he wasn't there to soften me up. Mainly what he was doing, from what I could tell, was making sure that the hospital was treating me well, that I was getting the care I needed.

My fight with the airline wasn't something particularly sensitive to tactics and strategy. Air New England assumed liability. I didn't have to prove to some hypothetical jury that the reason I couldn't walk wasn't *my* fault. Our lawyers would spend the next three years arguing over nothing much more than the size of the payout, which, all other things being equal in such cases, is a function of the size of one's salary. Rick and I didn't talk about how much money I did or didn't make.

The anger that washed over me the night of the crash waxed and waned during my stay in the hospital. It was ameliorated, certainly, by how happy I was simply to have survived, by the visits I received from the members of my family—I was as happy for them as for me—and by the endless rounds of entertainment that my hospital stay seemed to insist on providing. But it was never far below the surface. It came and went in flashes, the impossibility of my physical condition always there to feed it. Focused now on the airline in general—the Parmenter family, in its hour of grief, could do without judgment from me—the anger was never directed at Rick. He presented himself as an advocate, and taking him on those terms, I was grateful for his help.

The visit of his that I remember best was one of his earlier trips to South 2, the orthopedic floor on which my four-bed ward was located. Updating me on discoveries that investigators had made at the crash site, Rick, with a smile, informed me that they had found an ounce of marijuana in the debris. He wasn't being accusatory. Those on the scene had greeted the find with what Rick's lighthearted laugh would have me believe was an appropriate sense of humor. He wasn't going anywhere with the observation, just sharing a funny story. But everything in the way he said it told me he assumed the dope was mine.

He and probably everyone else.

In newspaper accounts of the crash, I was identified not simply by name, but as "the author of *Snowblind,* a candid view of the South American cocaine trade." There was a reason for this that had nothing to do with a desire to single me out, to ascribe to me any prominence. While I certainly thought of myself as somebody special, that belief was not widely held. The source of the attribution was Suzanne. Had it not been for Suzanne, I would have been described, if at all, simply as "a writer," much as, say, Paul had been described as "a medical student." Suzanne, however, in interviews she gave immediately after the tragedy, made regular mention of "the author" in her recounting of the escape: "I was sitting next to the author . . ." "When the author opened the door . . ." When Mary queried her at the airport, Suzanne said, "You mean the author?" She didn't say, "You mean Bob?" What Suzanne knew about me was what she remembered from the conversation we'd had before she reached across the aisle to tighten my seat belt. She might just as naturally have said, "You mean the guy who drives the three-liter BMW?" Quoting Suzanne in the news accounts, reporters had to clarify her remarks, had to explain what she meant by "the author." Once the description was set in type, it was treated like newspaper boilerplate and inserted into all subsequent stories along with my name.

Had I in fact been famous, referring to me as "the author Robert Sabbag," the way one would refer, for example, to the author Norman Mailer, would have been sufficient. But I wasn't famous that way, certainly not in Boston, despite its being my hometown. Nor anywhere else, for that matter. As I said, I was half a celebrity. Any notoriety I might have enjoyed, a substantial readership notwithstanding, was limited to certain small circles in New York and Los Angeles. I did get my share of fan mail, but a lot of it came from prisons. I wasn't famous in the typical way, nor was I ever likely to be. Even today, when almost everyone has a shot at celebrity, rarely is it thrust upon writers, and almost never on the basis of a body of work that consists of a single book, a nonfiction book at that. When the *Today* show appeared on the itinerary of the *Snowblind* promotional tour, I was taken aside by my publisher's director of publicity, who explained as kindly as possible that I was not being invited to appear. Host Jane Pauley's producers were interested in her talking not to me but to Zachary Swan. Seldom, over the course of several books, have I been interviewed as an author per se; invariably it is as a commentator on the subject of the book in question. It's true of most nonfiction writers.

Snowblind was always more famous than I. The book has been in print for thirty years, but even in the feverish days of my rise to visibility on the strength of it, my name meant nothing to most people, even to those who were inveterate readers.

Conversations that began "So, you're a writer?" had a way of changing course with mention of the book's title: "You wrote *that* book?" The subject matter of *that* book, in the absence of everything else, did have a way of ensuring that any mention of my occupation, at least for a time, would be followed by the kind of clarification evident in accounts of the crash. For the truth is that some people were not quite sure that I *was* a writer, not a real one, at any rate. Even today, *Snowblind,* in confused and erroneous references carried forward from the past, is occasionally referred to as an autobiography. People who hadn't read the book (whose main character, Zachary Swan, was born when Wyatt Earp was alive) and even some who had read it were quite prepared to believe that, rather than a reporter who had been commissioned to write the book, I was in fact a smuggler capitalizing on the one story I had to tell.

Not that I'm ungrateful for all the book brought my way. I recall attending a broadcast of *Saturday Night Live* in New York as a guest of comedian John Belushi. After the show and the party that followed, a group of us found our way to Studio 54. I was standing with Belushi's wife, Judy, when a cheer went up on the dance floor, raised in response to the sudden appearance of the nightclub's signature piece, a suspended Pop Art installation in the form of an animated crescent moon snorting cocaine from a spoon. As the two of us were laughing, I remember saying, "It's been very good to me." As true as that might have been at the time and as funny as we both found it—and despite the probability that she forgot it almost immediately—my having told her so is not something I look back upon with particular fondness. It wasn't very good to her. With the death of her husband three years later, cocaine would lose much of its charm and nearly all of its cachet.

But, nonetheless, I'd meant what I said. The dope business,

in its way, a wonderland colorfully populated by entertaining sociopaths, charmers, charlatans, cutthroats, comedians, out-on-the-fringe adventure junkies, and other adrenaline freaks, had provided the raw material with which I had launched a career. And I couldn't blame people like Rick, bringing news from the crash site, if they shared in the delusion that I necessarily had something in common with the characters whose adventures I'd chronicled. As I pointed out in a magazine piece that brought me some national attention recently, no one is more incredulous to learn that I don't smoke dope than those characters themselves. It's like asking them to believe that Damon Runyon didn't drink or hang out at the track. But they get over it after a while.

I hadn't been carrying pot on the plane, but I'd been carrying the proceeds of something that smelled a lot like it. While in New York, I'd borrowed some money. Five thousand dollars. I needed a quick infusion of funds to keep construction of the house going, and there was only one friend I knew I could count on to have the necessary cash on hand. It was a legitimate loan. I paid him back. How he earned the money I can only speculate. He worked in what he liked to describe as "the entertainment business." It was a description that the owner of Rick's recovered ounce would undoubtedly have found to be apt.

When I was wheeled into the emergency room, and they were about to scissor off my jeans, I asked if it would be possible to slide them off instead. Doctors seemed astonished, but were happy to oblige. I might have volunteered something stupid, like "this is my favorite pair." I didn't know what they might cut through, though I suppose now, in hindsight, that they're trained to avoid things like pockets, nor did I want anyone rifling through the jeans in preparing to throw them out. In one pocket, I was carrying exactly fifty grams of cash—in hundreds that the paramedic had put there; in another, I could have been carrying something that didn't weigh more than a few.

The doctors didn't get very far with me before Mary found her way into the emergency room.

"Hey, baby," I said, in a rush of excitement, lifting my head to greet her.

She placed her hand on my forehead, which made it effectively impossible for me to rise up off my back.

She said, "Don't do a lot of moving."

It was a trick I'd never seen before. Almost effortless on her part, but with all kinds of mechanical advantage. A nursing move. It was impressive.

"Take my jeans," I told her.

Smiling as though I were telling her how good it was to see her. We were all so hip in those days. I didn't have to say it twice.

During the summer months, Cape Cod Hospital operates the busiest emergency room in New England. It treats up to four hundred patients a day. Some 85,000 patients are treated there on an annual basis. The current emergency room, in use since 1993, saw its millionth patient in 2007.

The hospital, founded in 1920, has had a dedicated emergency department since 1950. I was treated in what is now referred to as the old ER, the upgrade that went into operation in 1976. The hospital's disaster plan, under which key department heads, medical staff, and ancillary personnel are notified and instructed to report for emergency service, was not implemented the night of the crash, but only because the time of the crash made it unnecessary, according to Ann Williams, who was the hospital's assistant director of community affairs.

"It happened at shift change," she told me recently, "and everybody was held."

Williams, who the following year would assume the director's job, received a call at home from nursing supervisor Virginia McLeod, who told her, "We think there's been a plane crash." Ten minutes later, McLeod called back saying the report had been confirmed. Williams arrived at the hospital at eleven-thirty and spent the next thirteen and a half hours handling inquiries. She said that in addition to dealing with the reporters gathered there, about twenty-five media people in all, she fielded "a thousand phone calls before one P.M.," when she finally left for the day.

"My big job was to keep the press out of the emergency room," she recalled.

Which didn't keep them from getting to me.

"This is summer," Williams reminded me. "We had to find a room for you."

It was on a table in the emergency room that I was notified that I had not been crippled for life. Up to that time, from the instant I stood up in the airplane, with my lower back telling me, "Stop right there," I confronted the possibility that it could go the other way. I didn't need a medical student like Paul to tell me—and I didn't bother informing him—that the people he was talking about who "shouldn't be moved" included me. With every step I took, moving about the cabin, each kick of the door, every inch I put between me and the wreck, I fought against discovering the answer to the inevitable medical question: At what point does a spinal injury become a spinal-cord injury? As relieved as I was to be alive, lying there in the woods, as happy as I was an hour later joking with the firefighters who carried me out, I knew I was facing a moment of truth. *Can you feel that? How about that? Good. How does that feel?* By the time Mary walked into the emergency room, I'd gotten the news. I don't think I'd been X-rayed yet, but at some point after the pictures came back, she explained the meaning of an L5 fracture, the injury that had kept me guessing.

"A compression fracture of the fifth lumbar vertebra."

"Compression fracture?"

"You broke your back. You'll be fine."

Once I had been treated, Mary rolled me out of the ER,

where I could light a cigarette without igniting the oxygen in use, and there in the hospital's main lobby, I met the assembled reporters.

"Sabbag refused to talk to anyone," the *Boston Globe* reported. "His wife, by his side, said little more. 'He's had a tough day. He was lucky' is all she would say."

The morning after the crash, Mary and the friend who had accompanied her to the airport were eating breakfast in a Hyannis diner. Seated nearby was a group of reporters, some of whom Mary recognized from our encounter in the hospital lobby. Now, with their stories filed, they simply nodded hello. Gone was the interest they had shown earlier in getting her on the record. With the passage of a few hours, she told me, she was literally "yesterday's news."

Even members of the press take themselves off the clock, and subsequent coverage of the crash would indicate that a sufficient number of journalists, writers as well as photographers, were on the job that morning. But Mary's observation is an interesting one and as good an introduction as any to a question that, while entirely hypothetical, nevertheless invites exploring: How would media coverage be different if the plane crash happened today?

In the present environment, one would see a difference, I think, not only in the scale of the response, but also in the occupational makeup of the personnel responding. Carried out of the woods today, it is reasonable to imagine, survivors would be met not simply by an array of satellite trucks but by a host of characters like would-be movie-of-the-week producers waving contracts for "life rights." The hospital would no doubt be home to a legion of segment producers employed by daytime TV. Families of the survivors, hustling to lawyer up, would be looking not only for personal-injury specialists but show-business attorneys as well. They'd be hiring literary agents.

It is not to say that the response that night was in any way genteel or the activity anything short of chaotic. It is not to suggest that the press on hand wasn't acting like the press.

Paramedic William Smith, carrying the middle sister out of the woods, remembers "giving the finger to reporters" as they converged on him and his patient, and he told me it wasn't the first time he'd done so in the four years he'd been on the job. His colleague Robert Jenney, a veteran EMT at the time, can still recount in detail a fight he had with one particular member of the media, a reporter he knew by name, an on-air guy for Channel 5, the ABC affiliate in Boston. "I had a problem with him," said Jenney, who retired in 1999 after more than thirty years in the fire department, explaining that he took the reporter on in defense of the youngest girl:

"Do you get turned on getting a picture of a ten-year-old all busted up?"

"Well, it's news, I have a right . . ."

"No, you don't have a right! Get out, or I'm calling the cops."

Today, in many parts of the country, there are cops and maybe a few firemen who would be signing deals with the media.

In the frenzy's immediate outbreak, Ann Williams said, her major concern and that of others on the hospital staff was for Doris Parmenter. The pilot's widow was known personally to many of the people on hand. She managed the hospital thrift shop. (The thrift shop was situated off-site, taking donations on Main Street in downtown Hyannis.) One of the better-connected journalists covering the crash was Francis Broadhurst, the news director for local radio station WQRC, and through sources only he was able to access, Broadhurst was the one reporter who knew that George Parmenter had been flying the plane. Broadhurst had been acquainted with Parmenter and had been friendly with Ann Williams "for years," having been involved with her in town politics in Barnstable, where Williams had served as chairman of the Finance Committee. Broadhurst, telling Williams what he knew, held on to the information until Doris Parmenter had been notified.

"If it happened today," Broadhurst told me recently, "there'd be a convention on her lawn. There would be photographers sneaking into the emergency room and taking pictures. Journalism's changed."

And with it, I think, something else has changed.

Tugging at the sleeves of every victim would be one of the insistent, altogether dysfunctional partners in the contemporary marriage of psychotherapy and the media.

I do not dismiss the value of therapy—I didn't question my fellow survivors about any help they might have sought—but I have trouble taking it seriously in the forum it has come to exploit. Individual therapy has measurable benefits, and I assume group therapy, in support of it, has its salutary effects. But therapy has lately transgressed the limits of the group, and grief and trauma counseling have gone public. Recovery today is entertainment.

In this, the age of information oversupply, the age of celebrity without delay, has the willingness to step forward opened us up to what is perhaps a more salubrious way of dealing with trauma? The experts tell me no. Such scrutiny so distorts the experience as to render any of the benefits of openness trifling. Talking does seem to come naturally at times, and in its way may be therapeutic, but such talk is not necessarily driven by a need for therapy; it's simply instinctive. Instinctive in certain circumstances. It's not instinctive in the company of strangers. War stories are rare even among intimates. Veterans, we know, don't talk to their spouses about combat. They don't share such memories with their children, not even, in my experience, when those children reach adulthood. All I know of what my father saw in the South Pacific I gleaned from the albums compiled by my mother of the photographs he had sent home with his letters, pictures more atmospheric of the Broadway musical of that name than of the drama that was playing out in places like Guadalcanal. War stories, when they are shared at all, are typically traded by comrades, understandable and fully explicable only when growing out of the common experience of brothers-in-arms. Coming from that guy sitting alone at the other end of the bar, they are a symptom of dissociative behavior.

"You run into guys, in various stages . . . they haven't left there yet," my friend Kevin Roberts tells me.

I've known Kevin for some thirty years now. We've experienced a lot together, most of it good, some of it bad, the worst of it his. There's not a lot we don't talk about. "There" is Vietnam, where he served with the U.S. Marines about fifteen years before he and I met. In all the years we've been friends, we've never talked about that. When he and other veterans cross paths, they don't talk about it much either.

" 'When were you there, where were you?'—and that's about as far as it goes. It certainly never gets into combat."

Calling upon such memories outside intimate circles is seldom rewarded, though there are circumstances in which doing so is entirely natural. In discussion of a plane crash reported in the news, or in discussion of air travel in general, I, for example, am not averse to bringing some perspective to the exchange of ideas.

"The reason she wants you to raise your seat back," I might

notify the argumentative passenger reclining in front of me, "is not for your safety, it's for mine. When the airplane crashes, and there's a pretty good chance it will . . ."

Stuff like that.

It's one of the few subjects on which my expertise is never challenged.

But opening up to the typical stranger or media personality, unbuttoning your shirt and letting your heart fall out before a television psychologist and the public at large, is neither instinctive in humans nor in any way natural and ultimately perverts the experience in a way that makes transcending it that much more difficult.

When I started looking back, one of the things that struck me as telling was that in over twenty-five years, none of us who had survived the crash (the three Michigan sisters being considered collectively) had been in contact with any of the others. I think that simply registering the thought shows how much things have changed. For on the most natural, human level, a reluctance to relive the experience, to subject it to the kind of public postgame analysis we bring to almost everything these days, doesn't seem unusual at all and never did, not to me or to the other survivors I talked to. Yet I believe it is unlikely that survivors today would similarly disperse never to see one another again. They would fall prey to external forces that didn't prevail at the time.

Denial, as it is commonly articulated, or that hobbyhorse of every therapist, "being defensive," may well be a response not to the traumatic experience itself, but to the impossibility of conforming the experience to what you perceive to be the expectations of others.

I can't speak for my fellow passengers—I offer it with no authority, and I'm really not sure myself, it's just an idea that won't let go—but I believe there may be something more to the inclination not to talk. *Especially* to one another. Despite the fact that nine of us came together to survive the crash, in one way, in its most primal way, it was *not* a group experience. In the end, survival never is. The trauma is so personal, so individual, and one's response to it is so solitary, that opening it up to varying interpretations threatens the equilibrium that each of us independently strives to recapture.

It probably started there in the woods, where we sat nursing our private fears, casualties propped up as in the pictures you see—though you couldn't see anything that night—of those Seventh Cavalry riflemen on the third day of battle in the Ia Drang Valley, strung out in the grass of the Central Highlands, the wounded waiting on MedEvac, each unwilling to wonder what the fight had forever taken away.

It's a suspicion I arrive at when I look back to the conversations I had with Paul and Suzanne. When I set out to revisit the crash, to ask others to relive the events of that night, I didn't know or try to guess what answers I might get. I didn't even know all the questions. I understood that I'd be finding my way, and I proceeded on faith that I'd light upon something of value, as difficult as those questions might be to answer. What I came away with was something I never expected: I never counted on how difficult those questions would be to *ask*.

Sitting down with Suzanne and later with Paul, I was startled by how awkward and inappropriate it seemed, how greatly the task I'd assigned myself differed from any I'd ever undertaken. I sat there with my notebook, the dutiful reporter; they sat dutifully entertaining my questions in the manner of cooperative sources. But this engineered formality defied the essence of our relationship, and in no way did it reflect the dynamic at play. Looking back to those conversations, I have to believe that the enterprise was somehow unbalanced by the weight of things I didn't really want to know.

Only now am I struck by a realization that eluded me then: They had no questions for me.

Maybe I shouldn't have been surprised that it was the one passenger who was separated from the group who recalled our waiting on rescue as a collective experience:

"Out there in the woods we were running out of things to talk about, back and forth," Jonathan Ealy said, when he and I spoke on the phone. "We're there, and the only thing we've got to keep us from collapsing is, 'Let's just keep the energy going so that we don't all disintegrate here.' The whole point for me, two things, one was just make sure I stayed in contact, in emotional contact, with you guys [who were] all together. The other was to make sure there was somebody over there in case . . . if the copilot got any worse, I was going to just yell for all the help I could get from anybody that could move. I was nineteen years old and I didn't want the guy to die with me supporting him from underneath."

When Jon had first appeared on our side of the airplane, everyone had been evacuated, and Suzanne had just made the decision to leave. "That was not my favorite decision of the evening," he told me. "I was pretty late to that party. I was a little steamed that a healthy-bodied person wasn't sticking around. . . . Everybody was so dinged up, and we needed to move people around. . . . If there had been a fire, in particular, we would have needed a lot of help with people who couldn't move."

Unknown to the rest of us, for whom activity had essentially ceased, there was a veritable opera being enacted on the other side of the aircraft, as Jon, for an hour and a half, in physical contact with the copilot, fought to keep him alive. "Minute-to-minute I was intensely involved in a relationship with a guy I didn't know."

Had Jon not wound up as he did, in front of the plane, it is almost certain that there would have been one less survivor of the crash.

"My nose was bleeding," he told me, and though, having broken it once before, he was used to the taste of blood, "it was really annoying," he said. "Later, the adrenaline wears off, everything starts hurting, my ribs start hurting—I wondered if maybe I'd punctured something—and then there's that taste and that smell of the blood and the fuel together. You know how smell is, it goes right down to the reptile brain. This is a memory I have at the most sort of primeval level. . . . At the end there, he was fading and I was clinging on to that tourniquet . . . it sapped all the energy away."

As a mechanism for putting trauma behind us, immediately or eventually, we are all naturally inspired to silence. It's almost as if one doesn't discuss these things in polite company. Putting words to a moment relived up to now only in silence does not come reflexively, nor does one approach it with any measure of ease. It is not something that suggested itself to me until thirty years after the fact, and I *have* a literary agent. It is only out of a generosity of spirit that those with whom I survived the crash came forward to help me, and nothing they might have said could more accurately have reflected the courage that was on display the night we first met.

A few years ago, I reported to Cape Cod Hospital for a minor outpatient procedure. In the course of prepping me for surgery, the nurse doing the intake vanished. It happened while I was momentarily distracted. The surgeon, the anesthesiologist, and others were coming and going, Pat was with me, she and I were talking, and I wasn't paying a lot of attention. I turned back in the nurse's direction, and sitting there, picking up where she'd left off, was the magician who'd orchestrated her disappearance, acting as though nothing had happened, behaving as if I were just one more patient and she just another of the several nurses on hand. I stood up, circled the instrument table, threw my arms around her, and laughed.

Her name was Mary Ellen, but introducing her to Pat, I didn't stop with that. Unsure of her marital status, I ventured all three of the last names by which I had known her when she and I were palling around. Now, twenty years since I'd last seen her, she was still going by the most recent of them, the product of a remarriage after which she and I had remained friends and largely in anticipation of which we had cut back on the palling around.

I'd met Mary Ellen at Cape Cod Hospital in 1979. We'd first laid eyes on each other on the morning of June 18. I was the guy in bed 209D.

"You were covered with jet fuel," she reminded me recently.

I had been admitted three or four hours earlier. She had just reported for work. They'd cleaned me up some in the ER, but I was only about as clean as a chimney sweep, still dressed out in what Mary Ellen remembers as a fine layer of soot.

"The first thing I did was wash your hair."

It wasn't the last thing she did.

Mary Ellen is one of the three or four nurses I remember looking after me that week. But as others came and went, she was the consistent presence, and for that and other reasons, she was special. When she wasn't there, I noticed it. Every day was a party with Mary Ellen, or that's how it seemed at the time. Maybe it was the smile with which she indulged the party I appeared to be throwing, clowning with all the offbeat acquaintances of mine who showed up on the ward, or maybe it was just a shared irreverence, but she and I would always find something to laugh about, and it is thanks to her that I can honestly say my being hospitalized was actually enjoyable.

A hospital is only as good as its nursing staff, and at the time of the crash, certain Cape residents, many of whom had never been treated there, took a perverse kind of pride in deriding the quality of care available at Cape Cod Hospital. Clearly they weren't paying attention. Today the hospital is rated among the top one hundred hospitals in the country, and back then you could see it coming. None of the nurses who treated me fell anywhere short of world class. I can't speak for the food. The crash had left me with a paralytic, or adynamic, ileus. Essentially what that meant was that my digestive system had called it quits, which was consistent with the trauma I'd sustained. An NPO order hung at the foot of my bed. Having graduated from the Boston Latin School (with grades that my best friend's mother was politely invoking when she assured me that "Every family needs at least one gentleman, Bob"), I knew that *nihil per os* meant "nothing by way of the mouth." Five days after I was admitted, my intestines resumed function, and I was put on a clear liquid diet. I don't recall eating solid food until after leaving the hospital. Four days into my stay, I celebrated with injections of Demerol while welcoming others to enjoy my birthday cake.

Mary Ellen is not the only nurse who dramatically affected my stay. First impressions being the most lasting, there is one other nurse I will never forget: the angel of mercy on duty Monday at four A.M., which was the time showing on the wall clock of the orthopedic floor when I was admitted. She may have been a supervisor. Before bedding me down on the ward, she wheeled me around the corner into the solarium where she permitted me to light up a cigarette. And I think it was she who engineered the accommodation that today makes me feel as if I were looking back over a century. Not simply did she allow me to smoke, she did it without admonishing me to quit, and then, without my requesting it, she took it upon herself to solicit from my ward mates the necessary approval that allowed me for the duration of my stay to smoke in the room, in bed—yes, a hospital bed.

O tempora, o mores!

In the week that I was hospitalized, my ward mates came and went. One of them, a teenage kid, or as the newspapers would have it, "a local youth," was the second patient to occupy the bed between mine and the window. He was admitted from the scene of a car crash. A good friend of his had been killed. He wasn't talking to anyone, not even his father, who visited regularly. A couple of days after he arrived, a state trooper, in uniform, showed up to question him. You could hear the creak of leather and the rattle of gear when he crossed the room, spit-polished from his boots to the peak of his combination cap. You could almost smell the gun oil and saddle soap. Walking up to the bed, he stood towering over the kid, radiating author-ity, the reflective surfaces of the tack and the hardware catching light from the window. Even I was intimidated, and he wasn't looking at me. He had questions for the kid about the car crash, and it was clear from the way he asked them that somebody had been lying about something.

The kid was alone, no parents, no lawyer, and I struggled with whether to tell him, "You don't have to say anything." I didn't want to make things worse, and I didn't want to get into a fight with the cop. It would have been a hell of a way to say thank you. The cop was one of the people whose job descrip-tion included saving my life a couple of nights earlier. As things progressed, it became clear to me that the kid didn't need my advice. To the extent that he was responsive, he was monosyl-labic, the same typically sullen, unsociable teenager that his father had found himself up against. He didn't give the trooper anything to work with.

The kid's dad was a character. I don't know what he did for a living. I had him figured for a workingman. He could have been an insurance guy or maybe an accountant, a generation removed from a working-class background, but something about him said blue collar to me. He was a lot like the peo-ple in my family, very much the kind of guy who'd be hanging around giving me advice when I was growing up. He seemed old enough to be one of my uncles, a little bit old, I thought, to be the father of a kid so young. He gave the impression of a man who'd come to parenthood late in life. His son wouldn't say more than a few words to him, so when he came to visit, he spent most of his time talking to me, or just keeping me com-pany. Or letting me keep him company. One day, when I wasn't really paying attention, he said one of those things that secured for him a permanent place in my memory. He was standing at the foot of my bed, talking to himself, it seemed, as much as he was to me, when I heard him say, "Bob, this is very good," and I glanced up to see him reading my chart. He nodded his head, looked up from the clipboard, and assumed me, "You're never going to have a problem with your blood pressure." I would forever take comfort in that, and never afterward would I think of my blood pressure without thinking fondly of him.

The morning I was admitted, there was a middle-aged fellow occupying bed B, the other windowside bed. I remember him for being the man who set me straight on the correct use of a term one encounters regularly on the Cape. I'd made the mistake of suggesting to him that with my recent acquisition of property, I was about to become a Cape Codder. He was the one who advised me—and all new arrivals can probably tell you from whom they received the advisory—that a Cape Codder is someone, and refers only to someone, who had the good sense to be *born* on the Cape. Those who wash ashore need not apply.

He himself, I believe, was one of the latter, and he was careful to make that fact clear. To read any class consciousness into his advisory is to be reading from outdated texts. The embrace of the Cape is all encompassing, blind to considerations of pedigree. Among its more festive traditions is the annual Blessing of the Fleet in Provincetown, when the bishop of the Catholic diocese travels out from Fall River to confer benediction upon the fishing vessels of Provincetown's largely Portuguese-American fleet. In celebration of the town's seafaring heritage, he stands at the end of MacMillan Pier casting protective aspersions of holy water on the procession of boats as it passes before him.

Provincetown Harbor, once home to sixty draggers, today supports no more than eight, only five of which are in working condition. David Dutra, captain of the oldest working vessel in the fleet, the *Richard & Arnold,* told the Provincetown *Ban-*

ner, "My boat was the biggest boat in Provincetown, it had a six-man crew, and now I fish it all alone. It's too much work for one man and not enough money for two." With the seas overfished and the town now reliant less on a maritime than a tourist economy, the Blessing of the Fleet has become but a small part of a larger Portuguese cultural festival, and the event is no longer the rowdy affair that it was thirty years ago. Held always around the first day of summer, the ceremony back then served as a rendezvous conspicuous for, among other things, the number of motorcycle enthusiasts it attracted. They set out for the Cape from all over the region to converge on Provincetown for the weekend. In the summer of 1979, one of them, in advance of his arrival, wiped out on the Mid-Cape Highway and wound up in the bed opposite mine.

Even without the injuries, as telltale as they might be, and stripped of everything but his hospital gown, he had biker written all over him. Everything about him shouted, "Too much ain't enough." It didn't take a lot to figure out: This was one of my readers. This was a guy who knew all the words to "One Toke Over the Line." And if my guess was right, it was his second-favorite railroad tune after "Casey Jones" by the Dead. A quick read on the guy when they brought him in, and I was ready to give odds that the people who were visiting me at the time weren't the only ones holding. Had the state trooper been on the ward that day, just one glance in the guy's direction, and he would have busted him for felony possession, without even shaking him down.

I know my public.

I don't think the biker was hospitalized for more than forty-eight hours, and I probably wouldn't remember him today but for the fact that he was a fan. The day he was released, his girlfriend—maybe she was his wife—showed up with his copy of my book, and I signed it for him as he was leaving. More than polite, he was actually rather bashful, and I doubt that it would have occurred to him, as it seldom does to readers, that when I autographed the book for him, the greater pleasure was mine.

The day my eyeglasses were delivered from the wreckage, Mary Ellen, horrified by their condition—"they were smeared with soot and fuel"—was thoughtful enough to clean them without making a point of it, wordlessly taking them from the bedside table, sparing me one more reminder of how I had wound up in her care. I didn't make a point of the fact that her name changed in the course of that week. From one day to the next, the surname printed on the ID tag she had been wearing was suddenly no longer in play. The logical inference was that she was shifting between a maiden and a married name. I didn't know her well enough to ask, but when I learned that she was the mother of an eight-year-old boy, I had a pretty good idea which way she was headed.

I have trouble separating what I learned about Mary Ellen in the course of my stay from what I learned about her after I was discharged. I can't say with any certainty how our personal friendship got started. I'm not sure that she and I made plans to be in touch when I was released. I remember receiving a phone call from her sometime the following year. She asked if I'd come see a patient, a guy a few years younger than I, who'd suffered a spinal cord injury in a rollover of his Jeep. It may have been around the friendship that he and I struck up that she and I got to know each other as well as we did. However it happened, she and I have been friends ever since.

It's not a friendship we nurture. We don't see a lot of each other. What makes it endure, I think, is that back when we saw each other more frequently, it was never less than fun. Without thinking about it, we observed a kind of check-your-blues-at-the-door policy that had taken its shape soon after we met. This was a woman who had managed to get me laughing within hours of my surviving a plane crash. The monkey business she pulled on the day of my outpatient surgery typified the nature of the companionship that had ensued thereafter.

By the time of my release from the hospital, Mary Ellen had moved my bed into the light of the window, which, among other things, afforded me a view. Mine was now bed B. The day before I was discharged, she walked into the room carrying crutches.

"On your feet," she said.

She helped me up out of bed and maneuvered me into a standing position for the first time since I'd escaped the wreck.

"Walk," she said.

And I did. Kind of.

"Try it one leg at a time."

She wanted to see me walk in what is known as a four-point gait, one crutch and the opposite foot moving forward sequentially, ambulating normally, in a natural, reciprocating stride, with the crutches merely providing stability. I was using what is called a swing-through gait, moving both crutches forward and then projecting my lower body between and beyond them. I didn't know any of this terminology at the time, but neither was I new to walking on crutches. Thanks to a couple of sports injuries and the manifestation when I was seventeen of a degenerative cartilage disorder of the knees that would eventually disqualify me from military service, I had spent a portion of my last three years in high school confined to crutches. I was pretty good at getting around on them. I'd seen people use them her way. My way, however, had the advantage of being faster.

"Give it a try," she said.

I gave it a try.

My way also had the advantage of being something I was able to do.

"OK," Mary Ellen said, "that's good. Back to bed."

She said it with a smile, as if my failing to master the four-point gait was a charming idiosyncrasy.

"I can't do it that way," I told her, as she walked me back across the floor.

"I can see that," she said, and smiled again.

I'd seen that smile before. Mary had it down pretty well. It's the practiced smile all nurses master early in their training, the polite and evasive smile they give you when the X-rays or the lab results come back, and they answer your question this way: "The doctor will be out to talk to you."

In this case, the doctor, an orthopedist, had apparently dismissed the evidence of the X-rays. And then Mary Ellen, after putting me on crutches, reported that I couldn't raise my right leg. That's when the doctor, my attending physician, a week after I'd been admitted, finally came around to noticing that my pelvis had been broken.

"I came in to gait-train you, and you couldn't walk," as Mary Ellen remembers it today.

I had been admitted with the previously described L5 fracture, with abrasions of both wrists, a large hematoma (subcutaneous swelling) of the left triceps muscle, and contusion and ecchymosis (internal bleeding) of the right groin. On my second day in the hospital, being treated for these injuries, I complained of pain in my lower abdomen. The orthopedist, in the clinical résumé that he later entered into my file, reported that I had "developed some lower abdominal pain and mild distention."

As a result, I was seen by a surgeon.

The abdominal pain wasn't acute, it was dull and throbbing, more an insistent discomfort, the kind of numb sensation you experience when the Novocain pumped into your mouth by a dentist starts to travel and your lower lip feels as if it's outgrown your face. When the surgeon asked me to describe the symptom, the closest I could come to nailing it down was to tell him, "My testicles feel like they're the size of an elephant's."

This prompted a smile, but I'm not sure if he smiled because he found what I'd said so funny or because what he was about to say was so much funnier. Speaking in a cadence distinctive of what I took to be an advanced education in Punjab, he made an observation that syllable for syllable is as entertaining as any I've heard from a doctor:

"Seldom do we find that to be cause for *complaint*," he said.

The emergency room X-rays of my right pelvis had been deemed normal by a radiologist and "essentially normal" by the intake physician. Reading new X-rays taken the afternoon of the surgical consult, a second radiologist guessed he was looking at a distended urinary bladder but would not rule out the possibility of a pelvic hematoma. X-rays were again taken the following morning. I have to assume this was done on the instructions of the surgeon, who unlike my orthopedist, would have been unsatisfied with the explanation, not because he was a surgeon, but because he was a good one.

Reading these last X-rays, the first radiologist found evidence of a possible "undisplaced acute fracture of the right superior pubic ramus," suggesting at the same time, however, that the cortical irregularity in question might simply represent an old break. My orthopedist took the optimistic view.

It didn't matter, anyway. My pelvis was busted, and the prescribed treatment was pretty much the same as the treatment

I was receiving for my broken back. But it was just one example of what I would come to see as a lack of enthusiasm on the part of my doctor, and it was enough for my old man.

My father, assigned to the navy's Hospital Corps, had received his commission while fighting in the Pacific. After the war, as an officer, he was assigned to the service's newly established Medical Service Corps. He spent the next twenty-two years of his military career—midway through which the navy put him through an Ivy League university—in hospital administration. At the time of his retirement, stationed at the Bureau of Medicine and Surgery in Washington, he was serving on the staff of the surgeon general of the navy. Remaining in the field as a civilian, he was the director of a hospital in Boston when I was laid up on the Cape.

My father had been answering to doctors and they to him pretty near all his life, and he held them in high esteem, but he didn't need to meet mine to know that Barnstable was a pretty small town of which Air New England was a pretty big part. What he knew from instinct and experience back then is born out by the record of treatment that I have before me now, and by the leap in the level of treatment I received once I was placed in the care of a physician more . . . let's say . . . energetic . . . than the orthopedist who had caught my case.

By the time I was discharged from Cape Cod Hospital, where my care was overseen by an otherwise excellent array of professionals and where the caliber of the admitting physicians today is extremely high, my father had lined up an orthopedist in Boston. It was this doctor who ordered the X-rays that showed that the pain developing in my upper back, the pain that ten years later in Santa Barbara drew Gael's curiosity, was being referred down from a displaced cervical vertebra. This was the source of the discomfort I would continue to live with long after the injuries to my pelvis and lower back had healed.

While they are somewhat easier to talk about than the subtler and often more serious psychological effects of such trauma, the physical injuries I sustained in the plane crash do not reward a lot of scrutiny. What little I've said about them here is more information than I've communicated to anyone, more information than I've communicated to everyone, in the years since they occurred. Charting the progress of one's physical incapacitation is an indulgence I associate with the more sedentary residents of Sunbelt retirement communities. A staple in their conversational diet, it is not my cup of tea. Perhaps it's the way I was raised. I'm no more likely to participate in the exercise when they throw me in a wheelchair than I was when I was a kid. Apart from maybe allowing that I'd rather not sit under a ceiling fan, where the draft might stiffen my neck, I'm no more apt to raise with you the subject of the arthritic changes afflicting my upper back than to share with you the current state of my kidney or bowel function.

But there is something to this other than upbringing. It is something I learned relatively early in the course of my recuperation, when stuck between the eagerness to get back up on my feet and the necessity to inventory my losses for the purposes of compensation. And it saved me a lot of heartache. Somebody— it may have been my lawyer—sat me down and gave me some of the best advice I was ever lucky enough to receive. And now I'll give it to you: There is nothing more debilitating than to think of yourself as a casualty. To measure yourself in terms of your inadequacies, to keep pausing to monitor your losses, is more than psychological quicksand, it is physically unhealthy. Not until I was free of that kind of thinking would I be able to regain my strength.

Itemizing your deficiencies is no way to live your life. I was bred to believe this from childhood, but it was something I had to relearn. That I happened to get beat up in a plane crash was just one more of those things the world served up over which I had no control. That's how I came to see it. It was of no more passing importance, I decided, than the fact that I'd suffered bronchitis as an infant or that I happened, say, to be near-sighted. I'm not as tall as I'd like to be either. I'm more dashingly handsome than Robert B. Parker, and there's plenty more where that came from. I fall asleep counting my blessings.

A word about compensation. Americans will more readily volunteer their medical history than talk to you about their money. I don't know what kind of settlements my fellow survivors reached with the airline. I didn't bother to ask. I wasn't interested in the numbers, and I knew everything I needed to know about the experience. Theirs would have been no different from mine in any way that was instructive. The claim to which I was a party, thanks to the caliber of the advocates on both sides, was handled in as dignified and professional a manner as such endeavors ever enjoy. And still, there was nothing enriching about it. There are few things that come with greater spiritual cost than involving yourself in a lawsuit. No matter how successful you emerge, the trade-off is never worth it. All they give you is money. And in liability cases, to make serious money—if that's what you're after—what you really want to do is die. Mine was a case where proving liability was unnecessary. I was well represented, in the end I was treated fairly, and it was three years of my life you can have. Damages are compensatory, an indemnity, not a reward. You keep the cash. I'll take the no-plane-crash option.

The NTSB, in its findings, reported that when the plane hit the woods, "Two passengers were not wearing their lapbelts." Neither passenger was identified by name. One, of course, was Jonathan Ealy, who had been thrown through the cockpit on impact. I'd known that within a couple of days of the crash, advised of it by the federal investigators who visited me in the hospital. The other was Brian McCann, the passenger lying in the aisle beneath the seat to which I was strapped when the plane came to rest. I wouldn't know that until almost thirty years later.

Tracking down my fellow survivors, I took advantage of contemporary information technology. One might say that the task would have been nearly impossible before development of the Internet search engine, but to believe that is to believe in fairies.

My first job, right out of college, was as a reporter for a now defunct Scripps-Howard newspaper, the *Washington Daily News*, an afternoon tabloid that competed for circulation with two broadsheets in the nation's capital, the *Washington Post*, which is still in business, and the *Evening Star*, which is not. The *News* will forever be famous for having been home to the legendary Ernie Pyle, the Pulitzer Prize–winning war correspondent who lost his life on Okinawa. When I went to work at the *News*, almost a quarter of a century after he died, Pyle's desk was still in the newsroom and little had changed since he'd last used it.

Stories at the *News* were generated in a city room that even then was a primitive artifact of American industry. Lifted intact and hauled away, it could have been placed on exhibit in a wing of the Museum of History and Technology at the Smithsonian. Copy, composed on manual typewriters, was edited with pencil, paste pot, and scissors. Rolled and stuffed into cylinders, it was delivered by pneumatic tube from the city desk to keyboard operators downstairs, whose clattering typesetting machines spit out lines of justified type in the form of hot slugs of cast lead.

It was a place where a young reporter could follow a story's physical transformation as it went from the pages of his notebook to the pages of a newspaper leaving the building in the back of a truck. The story, within a couple of hours of the time it was written, would appear under his byline alongside a cup of coffee on Capitol Hill, or a beer and a shot across the street. Deadline for the city edition was seven A.M. The paper, rumbling off the web-fed presses, hit the street at nine. It was a time when, unless you arrived in handcuffs, you needed a necktie to get into court. Some of the old-timers still owned fedoras, and even the female reporters wore trench coats. A cigarette habit, though not required, was a pretty big part of the deal.

All a reporter needed in the way of a search engine back then was a phone, a cross-directory, and a morgue. After that it was just a combination of shoe leather and no shame. A newspaper morgue is an archive of stories clipped from previous editions of the paper. The morgue at the *News* was a small room behind the city desk choked with file cabinets containing ages worth of yellowing newsprint and original black-and-white glossies. A cross-directory is a listing, arranged alphanumerically by street, showing the name and phone number of the current resident at any given address. (And the names and numbers of that resident's neighbors.) A telephone . . . Well, the newer telephones at the *News* were the rotary-dial phones that weren't black. With these tools, a standard phone book, and the right number at the Department of Motor Vehicles, a reporter at any newspaper, like all the private eyes in pulp fiction, could find any person he wanted to talk to. Today the same reporter would type the name of that person and click "Search."

In finding people who were present that night in 1979, I started with a morgue that was no more sophisticated than the one I'd used at the *News*. It consisted of the stories I'd clipped from the newspaper while I was confined to the hospital in the days after the crash. The clips, yellow with age and few in number, contained the names of numerous people I would eventually talk to, but they were of no practical value to me in tracking down the survivors themselves. The names of the survivors, where they were from, their ages, their occupations, the schools that some were attending, the simple biographical bullet points by which they were identified in the newspaper—over the years I had forgotten none of it. I could repeat the information in my sleep. Sometimes I did.

Brian McCann was eighteen years old, a student at Boston College. He was from New Rochelle, New York. He broke his collarbone in the crash. That's what the newspaper had said, and all of it had remained with me. I knew more about him than that. I knew what his nightmares were like. I remembered things he would never forget. But to find him I had only what I knew from the newspaper, and it was all I needed to know.

To say that McCann is a common name—and granted, I grew up in Boston—is to my mind akin to suggesting that Marie Antoinette liked to shop. It's certainly more common than my name. And few are the McCanns, I would submit, who have not at one time or another considered the name Brian for that bundle of joy on the way. The Catholicism of the Irish, I think, tends to hasten the inevitable. With six or seven trips to the maternity ward . . . Sean, Michael, Patrick . . . sooner or later, it's going to be Brian.

(As I would discover, the Brian McCann I was looking for was one of eleven children in his family, ten of whom were boys, an accomplishment that even my parents, who ushered five children of their own into the insatiate bosom of the Catholic Church, might have perceived as showing off.)

In trying to find the Brian McCann who that night had mistaken his broken collarbone for a dislocated shoulder, I launched a preliminary electronic search, prepared for battle in a war of attrition with all the Brian McCanns of the world. I never anticipated being overwhelmed by just one of their legion's number: Atlanta Braves catcher Brian Michael McCann, a 2006 National League all-star , who in 242 at bats that year went .333, with 34 doubles, 24 homers, and 93 runs batted in. There was no escaping the guy. Or his stats. In the time that it would have taken me to extract from the search enough data to narrow its parameters, in the time required to circumnavigate that single entry, only to reach the virtual armada of Brian McCanns certain to lie beyond, I could have driven to New Rochelle.

By coupling today's technology with the old-fashioned skills I had picked up as a reporter, I saved myself the drive. The alumni associations of most universities, Boston College being one of them, are accessible on the World Wide Web. But in almost every case they are accessible exclusively to the alumni themselves. An investigator, any police detective will tell you, is only as good as his informants, and over the years, I have managed to cultivate some excellent confidential sources. It's not how I usually think of my dental hygienist, Sue, but her son, as luck would have it, attended Boston College. Within twenty-four hours, I had the addresses of more than one Jesuit-educated Brian McCann, and among them was a student who had graduated three years after the crash. He lived in Connecticut.

He recognized my name, with no reference to the crash, when I introduced myself over the phone. Sparing me the burden of an awkward preamble, for which I was grateful, he made a joke about airplanes. He agreed to meet me to discuss what he called "a life-changing event," but rather than open up time in his schedule in Connecticut or in Manhattan, where he worked as a currency trader, he preferred to meet on the Cape.

That he still remained somehow attached to the Cape came as no surprise. Cape Cod is not really a moveable feast. It does not stay with you that way. It is not like Paris so much as like Lourdes. Being there is the important thing. It is more like a reliable dope connection: People keep coming back. Guessing that Brian's family, like Suzanne's, had probably had a summer place on the Cape at the time, I asked where he had been going when the plane crashed.

"I was going to see my sister," he said, explaining that she still had a home in Brewster, that he continued to visit her there, and that he was planning to do so soon, at which point he and I could meet. He asked if I knew Brewster. I told him I did.

He said, "You know the general store?"

It was where everyone met.

"I know it well," I said.

The Brewster Store, built as a church in 1852 by members of the Universalist Society, was converted to a general store in 1866, and through a succession of five owners, it has been operated as such in the mid-Cape town for which it is named for almost a century and a half. General stores are a common feature of Cape Cod, which remains, in its own way, rural, but few match the store in Brewster for atmosphere and charm, and none succeeds so well in preserving a feeling of never having changed. The sense of continuity is reflected in the assortment of merchandise available and in numerous antique appointments, many of which are in everyday function, including a peanut roaster, a turn-of-the-century nickelodeon, and an old coal stove in the middle of the store around which patrons sit and warm themselves in winter. The wide steps of the front porch, which are perfect for loitering, and the painted benches outside, which were installed by the current owners to extend the capacity for same, give the two-story, wood-frame structure on Main Street a center-of-town flavor in a town that has no discernable center.

Owners George and Missy Boyd bought the store in 1986— they have owned another Brewster business longer—and it was just a few years before they bought it that they and I became acquainted. We met in New York through mutual friends, Robert Billingsley and his wife, Janice. Bob Billingsley and I will have known each other for half a century soon, and our friendship, which runs deep, is of a rare and special character, one of "the kinds of friendships," says Hillary Clinton, who is married to another of my college classmates, "that have to be rooted in the common experiences of one's youth." I've known Janice almost as long.

The Boyds and the Billingsleys, whose daughters attended the same school in Manhattan, are more than friends, they are the kinds of friends who spend family holidays together. My acquaintance with the Boyds, springing as it does from my long friendship with Bob and Janice, is such that when I see them, it usually happens in New York rather than on the Cape, where I now spend most of my time. A typical example of our getting together was a small birthday party the Billingsleys hosted in their Upper West Side apartment to which the three of us were invited.

Ghosts, once laid to rest, will remain there undisturbed, effectively forgotten, neglecting to reveal themselves even over the extended course of the most intimate friendships. I had known the Boyds casually for some twenty-five years, had seen and talked to them on almost as many occasions, and had talked to the Billingsleys over that time almost as often as I'd talked to the members of my family, before I learned that Missy Boyd's maiden name was McCann and that the young man I'd helped to his feet that night as I rose to my own in the wreckage of the aircraft was her brother.

"Your sister owns the Brewster Store?"

"She didn't own it then."

"Missy Boyd is your sister?"

And that is just one of the synapses across which the signal had never been transmitted.

The eleven McCann children had grown up in New Rochelle within a block of another, equally energetic family of Irish Catholics, one of whose twelve children, Brian informed me, lived in Wellfleet and owned a business there. Brian asked if I knew him. "Pretty well, in fact," I said. Older than Brian, younger than I, he was someone I had met and become friendly with two years after the crash. I had known him for twenty-five years, Brian had known him since childhood, and never in all that time, on either side of the mutual acquaintance, did the connection the two of us shared reveal itself.

Again, it's as if these were not the kinds of things one talked about in polite company.

"It's a small world," observes comedian Steven Wright, "but I wouldn't want to paint it."

Well, he needn't bother. The phenomenon that sociologists and mathematicians refer to as the small-world problem has driven enough academic dissertations to wallpaper it. A hypothesis of social networks that has been around for almost a century, small-world conjecture puts forward the idea that any two randomly selected people will exhibit a connection to each other through a chain of associations that includes six other people, on average. The idea took hold in popular culture under the label "six degrees of separation," after the 1990 play of that name by John Guare.

I'm naturally skeptical of this kind of gibberish, but then I was never very good at math. Given my connection to Missy Boyd by way of her brother Brian, Paul's connection to Parmenter by way of a shared relationship to both Wendy and Grover Farrish, Suzanne's connection to Jim Bernier by way of an acquaintance with me, and yet another, similar connection, revealed to me later, between an alarm technician and a caretaker who crossed paths at a summerhouse in the town of Chatham—all of whom had been present on the night of the tragedy, separated in each case by a single degree—I was becoming something of a believer. And my susceptibility was exacerbated by the nagging realization that I was likewise separated from Guare himself, the dramatist who popularized the phenomenon and gave it a name, only by the professor under whom we both studied playwriting in college.

When I finally reached Jonathan Ealy in Anchorage, he confirmed that he had graduated from the Duke University School of Law in 1985. That they might not have recognized each other is understandable, considering the circumstances of their original meeting, but it's a good bet that Ealy, crossing the Durham campus, occasionally nodded hello to Paul Boepple, who was doing his pediatric residency there at the same time.

More than four months passed between the evening Brian and I talked on the phone and the day we finally got together. He and his family—his wife, a fashion consultant, and two daughters, ages eleven and fourteen—were visiting Missy in Brewster, and he took a morning out of his vacation to keep an appointment with me. We met at the general store on a Monday in early July. It was eight A.M., and the place was busy. It was the start of the tourist season on Cape Cod. Everything was picking up. The sun was shining, and along with several of the Boyds' other patrons, Brian and I sat on the benches out front sipping carryout coffee.

Clean-cut, athletically built, he still had a youthful air about him. He was wearing blue jeans, a T-shirt, and Top-Siders, but he's one of those people who can wear anything—he would have looked just as laid-back in a suit. He appeared to be a guy who took care of himself, and everything else about him told me he was probably pretty well fixed, something I'd first suspected when I came across his address. His hair had grayed, but he had all of it, and his haircut cost more than mine. In addition to the sense of humor I'd first picked up from him over the phone, he had all the confidence and sophistication you'd expect to find in an educated guy who negotiated the international currency markets out of an office in midtown Manhattan. It says something about me, not about him, that a part of me reacted as one might to a younger brother who'd gone out and done well for himself. My arithmetic put him at forty-seven years old.

He was the third survivor I talked to, and he was the first to express curiosity about the injuries I'd sustained in the crash.

"I didn't realize you were hurt that bad," he said.

His memory was that I'd been pretty active.

"Not for long," I assured him.

He was treated that night at the emergency room and released with a broken collarbone. Thirty-six hours later, he was carried from his sister's house on a stretcher and taken back to the hospital, where he was diagnosed with a hip pointer, which is a contusion of the iliac crest, the bony prominence that can be felt along the waistline. Following X-rays, he was released with pain pills. (I don't know who initially treated him, but I'm guessing we shared an orthopedist, who, while undoubtedly having attended medical school, was apparently absent the day they covered the pelvis.)

He remembered the moment of impact in detail.

"It was a long ten minutes," he said, of the interval between the landing announcement and the plane's ultimate contact with the trees. "I heard stuff hitting the bottom of the plane. . . . The lights blinked. I remember thinking, *I'm about to die.*"

Then came the sound of the crash.

"I just let go. I said, *This is it.*"

Thrown into the aisle, facedown on the deck (he was the first thing I saw when my vision cleared), he continued his inner monologue as the plane came to rest.

"I remember asking myself, *Am I dead?*"

He had his answer within seconds:

"I tested my limbs. . . . *I'm still alive.*"

And the first voice he heard was not that of God.

I remember asking him if he was OK and helping him up off the floor. As soon as it was clear he could walk, the evacuation began.

Brian confirmed that it was he who had helped carry the eldest sister from the plane. "She was a mess," he said, and he remembered that "her legs caught on the door" as he carried her through. "Yes," he verified, "she was unconscious. We didn't take her far."

It was unquestionably Suzanne with whom Brian had carried the young woman to the rear of the cabin—Suzanne remembers her being hot to the touch—and whether it was Suzanne or the middle sister with whom he carried her off the plane, he remembered that he and the middle sister walked away from the craft together. He stayed with her, not the eldest, as we settled in, waiting to be rescued, her head leaning against his chest as we huddled in the dark. Her injuries were not visible either to Brian or to me, but being extremely talkative, she exhibited sufficient distress to indicate that she was suffering from shock. In fact, her injuries were such that upon arrival at the hospital, she was admitted.

The middle sister and the youngest had been seated on the right-hand side of the cabin, just aft of the cockpit bulkhead, the youngest sitting on the inboard side. Behind them, in a string of double seats, in order of proximity, sat Jon, Brian, Suzanne, and Paul. The left-hand side of the aircraft, the pilot's side, was lined with single seats. The two people seated on that side of the cabin were the eldest sister and I. She was sitting up front. Our side had taken the worst of the impact. The cockpit on our side of the plane was destroyed. Crushed four feet back on the other side, it was crushed nine feet back on our side, torn away along with the bulkhead and a portion of the front cabin, the area in which the young woman was sitting and into which her youngest sister's seat extended.

The oak tree standing inside the airplane had passed through the captain's position. Sometime during the crash sequence, his restraint system had released and he was ejected from the cockpit. His body was found twenty-five feet forward of the wreckage. The failure of his harness, triggered by impact damage to the buckle, did not influence his chances of survival. His fatal injuries, according to the government crash report, "were caused by trees impacting the left cockpit and by the collapsing cockpit structure as the aircraft descended through the trees."

Brian, going into his sophomore year at Boston College, survived the crash to celebrate his nineteenth birthday in July. His brother Bill was married three weeks after the crash, and at the wedding, Brian received a standing ovation.

"It's always what *could* have happened," he told me. "It affects the people not involved more than the people involved."

His brother Denis had driven him to the airport that night, and seeing Brian after the crash, "he couldn't speak" for a few seconds. "That close . . . What *if?*" were the first words he uttered.

Such moments, Brian said, undercut all his bravado.

"You say it's no big deal, but it *is* a big deal. You appreciate them, the family, that much more."

In helping me recapture a fuller sense of that night, an appreciation of events as perceived through the prism of his experience, Brian punctuated the conversation with what he identified as "remarkable moments." And virtually all of them concerned his family: "the love in her voice" when he first talked to Missy; his brief call from the hospital "to let my family know I'm alive"; and his father, "not a touchy-feely guy," carrying it all in the sound of his voice, the weight of all that emotion, when he told Brian, "We're on our way."

Hearing these things in the context of what I knew about the McCann family served to verify my belief in the therapeutic quality of love.

Bob and Janice Billingsley, who spend every Christmas Eve with the Boyds, attending church with them in Manhattan, know Missy's family not only to be close-knit but also to be very tightly tied across generational lines. "When you go to a party at Missy's, the entire family is there," says Bob, who has attended gatherings at the Boyds' apartment in Manhattan. "I have met all her brothers and sisters-in-law and all the nieces and nephews, all the relatives, even the cousins." And the familial bond is mirrored in another kind of unity that he finds remarkable. "They all look alike. Try to guess which ones are her brothers, and you'd get eight out of ten."

In the summer, the entire family heads en masse to the Cape.

"Everybody, all eleven people and all their children go to Missy's on the Fourth of July." Missy, the second oldest of the eleven children, the only daughter, is "the family matriarch," Bob says. "To understand the family is to understand her." Janice describes the July get-together as a "three-or-four-day" affair, an extravaganza marked by pageants and skits in which the children are expected to perform. Missy's orchestration of the event is a long-standing tradition that Janice sees as part of "the glue that pulls the family together." And there is no question, she says, that "the family being so accessible helped get [Brian] through."

In as many ways as not, the story I was unearthing was a story about families, and what moved me most about Brian's experience was how familiar it seemed, how accurately it reflected mine, and how for me, as for him, an appreciation of that night would have been inexpressible from any frame of reference that did not include the members of my family.

O ptimism is a blessing that was conferred on me at birth. It has been a lifelong article of faith with my mother that "Things always work out for the best." Hearing her say it when I was growing up was as predictable as hearing "Don't forget to brush your teeth" and "Call us when you get there."

I was no older than eleven or twelve when I learned the meaning of the word *optimist*. The first time I remember hearing the word was when my aunt Julia, my father's sister, applied it to me. "I see you're an optimist," she told me, one Sunday at her home in Boston, walking up behind me and looking over my shoulder while I sat at her dining-room table solving a crossword. "What's an optimist?" I wanted to know. "Someone," she said, "who does crossword puzzles in ink." I confess that, for at least a while thereafter, I believed it to be the literal definition, as if the English language were so all encompassing as to have a word for someone who did that:

So what do you do for fun, Bob?

I like to play baseball, and I'm also an optimist.

You can find *optimist* defined, as I eventually did, in a dictionary, but you will look in vain to find a more splendid embodiment of the word than my mother. Well into my adulthood, Easter remained one of the holidays on which the entire family gathered, my brothers and sisters and I traveling to my parents' house from wherever we happened to be to observe the occasion together. It was also a holiday on which one of the big-screen Bible epics depicting the life of Christ could inevitably be found on television, and whether it was *The Robe* or *The Greatest Story Ever Told,* it was a broadcast my mother seldom missed. It is safe to say that, on the occasion of the Easter story I'm about to tell, my mother had seen the movie in question about twenty times. And she'd been familiar with the source material since long before the film was made. It was the life of Jesus. She'd read the book.

It was sometime in the afternoon that Terry and I, while we were talking, heard a cry of distress from my mother, who was busying herself in the kitchen. We turned to look in on her. We asked if she was OK. She was sitting at the table with a paring knife in her hand. The television was on, and whatever she might have been slicing was receiving only half her attention. My mother, ever conscientious, always careful not to alarm, was quick to assure us that she was fine, but from the disappointment in her voice, it was evident that something was wrong.

"What is it?" Terry wanted to know.

My mother sighed. She shook her head.

She said, "They picked Barabbas."

They, the multitude in the movie on television, they'd shouted, "Give us Barabbas!" choosing him over Jesus when they were asked by Pontius Pilate, the empire's man in Judea, which of the two biblical troublemakers deserved to have his sentence commuted.

I looked at Terry, who looked right back at me. Her smile said, *You're surprised?* I asked my mother the question to which Terry and I both knew the answer.

"Did you think it was going to go the other way?"

The three of us were laughing now.

"No . . . no," she said. My mother has a way of laughing and showing frustration at the same time. "But . . ."

But nothing. My mother was really holding out hope that it might be different this year. She really believed, somewhere deep in her heart, that if things broke her way, the multitude might actually pick Jesus this time, that two thousand years of Christian history would still play out just fine if Rome, laying a foundation for what the Church would one day recognize as the spiritual acts of mercy, had slapped Jesus with a desk-appearance ticket, maybe hit him with something like a D felony, rather than crucify him.

I know exactly what she was thinking, because it's the way I tend to think, too. Or did. Until that night in the woods. After that, I think, at least for a while, my innate optimism went south, along with some of my confidence.

My father, a practical man, who'd come to terms early in life with the idea that Jesus had been crucified, was no less openhanded than my mother in the dispensation of positive thinking. While my mother administered the optimism, he wrote the prescriptions for confidence. That confidence translated as often as not into blissful ignorance on my part, but ignorance, I submit, of an indispensable kind, the naive sort of arrogance that enabled me, for example, to just up and write a book. It simply never occurred to me that it couldn't be done. I never entertained the thought that I would (as I did) encounter anything that as a writer I hadn't come up against, even though, until then, I'd never reported a story that had run much longer than five hundred words.

But more than confidence in my ability to succeed, he gave me confidence in my ability to prevail. I cannot remember the circumstances, but at some disheartening moment in my life, I was sharing my misgivings with him, and what he said to me in response to my troubles he framed in such a way as to make the words self-fulfilling. He said quite simply that I shouldn't worry about it too much (whatever it was that was bothering me) and by way of telling me why assured me that *he* wasn't worried.

"You always seem to manage to land on your feet," he said.

He didn't say it as though trying to encourage me. He said it as though sharing a secret, the way another parent might say, "You're adopted." As if it were something I had no control over, something I couldn't escape. He was simply sharing an observation, a conclusion anyone else might reach.

There are moments in the lives of all of us when the words we need to hear at the time have an impact that is way out of proportion to their everyday throw weight, and this was going to be one of them. There is nothing—no weapon, no wind or vaccine—with the power to match the naked, instrumental might of simplicity, and that simple observation ventured by my father somehow gained the force of prophecy.

It was not something I'd ever thought about. But to doubt it would have been to doubt *his* success, for he was the one who'd equipped me with whatever capability I had. It is the responsibility of all parents to instill in their children the heart needed to prevail, and my father was no doubt speaking out of a certain pride in himself when he pointed to what he perceived, and wanted me to perceive, as my ability to land feetfirst.

But that belief in myself—and my optimism along with it—took a dark turn after the crash. I can see it now, looking back. After the crash, I found myself, when things were going well, just waiting for them to go sideways.

Mary had a different way of looking at the tendency that my father had led me to have faith in. And her reminding me of it was a bit more left-handed:

"Bob, you'll always be lucky."

Not until after the crash was it a tendency for which I felt an apology was necessary.

There's nothing wrong with being lucky, and there's a lot of truth in the belief that we tend to make our own luck. But after the crash, being told I was lucky was something I didn't want to hear. The notion that I would always wind up on my feet, the proposition that had been my ally for so long, now presented itself as the enemy. I could not escape the idea that somehow I was *just* lucky, that I didn't earn my luck or, more important, deserve it. And any suggestion that I had luck on my side—however it was intended—just reinforced the symptom. It wasn't a symptom I necessarily recognized, certainly not a feeling I recognized for what it was. But it was a feeling that could only have flourished in the fertile soil of what I would come to understand to be the syndrome known as survivor guilt.

Hospitals, I guess, are like prisons. One of the things you pick up from convicts, an observation you're not apt to make if you've never done time yourself, is that in lockup, they never shut off the lights. Not all the way. It's how the people keeping an eye on you keep an eye on you at night. Inmates, who by definition don't see much of the sun, never enjoy the benefits of darkness either. You have to wonder if there's a flourishing market in a hellhole like San Quentin in those little courtesy packets they hand out on airplanes that contain sleep shades and earplugs. I didn't notice it at the time, or let's say I didn't find it conspicuous, but as I lay in bed in the hospital, comforted by narcotics, there was no part of the ward or the hallway beyond it that was not at least dimly illuminated. So it wasn't until nightfall of the day I was released that I discovered I was afraid of the dark.

When you say it like that—the Dark—it has an almost metaphysical ring to it. It smacks of eschatology, like something out of Revelation, something unknowable hiding in the second law of thermodynamics. I mentioned it to Suzanne. Yeah, she said, me too. She just said it. We didn't discuss it. It passed. It was like the flu. Me, I slept with the lights on for a few days and was careful for a while thereafter not to be outdoors at night. Brian said he experienced it also. It seems to have passed as quickly for him. What didn't pass that quickly, he told me, were the nightmares.

"I had nightmares through college," he said. "I still have dreams about planes crashing."

But the nightmares were not the worst of it.

"The magnitude of something like that," he said, "that you could get up and walk away. I didn't think I was supposed to be here."

By which he meant, to be alive.

"I had survivor guilt for several months," he said.

Survivor guilt, once a specific diagnosis, is now recognized in the medical literature as an associated symptom of posttraumatic stress disorder (PTSD). Diagnosed in those who have escaped horrors in which others have been killed or seriously injured, it expresses itself in feelings of sadness and shame, a debilitating sense that one really shouldn't be alive. Because it is largely limited to mortal events, the term can be misinterpreted. Or so my experience suggests. It is not always the death of others for which you necessarily feel guilty. Death is just the fundamental reminder of what was supposed to happen to *you*. It triggers the Why not me? response that leads you to believe you *should* have died, the weird notion that in some way you had an obligation to do so, that you don't really deserve to live. Not only is your survival unfair to the dead, it is unfair to the living as well. You have no right to be that lucky.

"Why am I still here?" was the question Brian asked himself when his nightmares awakened him.

It was not an ontological question, but at least he gave it voice. I don't remember asking it. I just remember being prepared for the worst. However well things were going, there was always something to fear.

"I'd wake up in the middle of the night," Brian said, feeling that "I dodged a bullet. There's another around the corner."

The feeling, he said, lasted through Christmas.

Kevin Roberts carried the same feeling around with him for just about thirty years.

"Why am I constantly in fear that the bottom is going to fall out, and I'm going to end up tomorrow on skid row?" was the question that haunted him, convinced, as he was, that "whatever the worst is, it will happen."

Kevin is the friend who told me that when he and fellow veterans talk, they never talk about combat. We were sitting on the beach in Eastham below the vacation cottage he and his wife had rented, as they did every summer with the kids. It was the middle of the day, and the tide was in, pushing us back to the edge of the dune on which the two-week rental was situated. It was a perfect day to be on Cape Cod Bay, and while everyone else was enjoying it, he and I had found a quiet spot to discuss all the terrible things that keep people up at night.

I knew precisely what Kevin was talking about when he mentioned asking himself why he was always in fear of the worst. The answer for him, as it was for me, was, Well, because you deserve it. It's that metaphorical bullet you dodged. But Kevin's PTSD was complicated by more than survivor guilt.

"I was never afraid, all the time I was there," he told me, of his tour of duty in Vietnam. "That's a symptom of PTSD. Not talking about it is a symptom of PTSD."

He waited thirty years before seeking therapy, and had been in therapy for a full two years, when his therapist said this:

"Wait a minute . . . you were in Vietnam?"

It had never occurred to Kevin to mention it.

"I hadn't gotten over the nuns yet," he told me. "And a whole lot of other things . . . 'Oh yeah, Vietnam, maybe that too. . . .' By the time you're in your fifties, there's stuff in there that's pretty hard-wired . . . 'I'm not special.' It goes back to the nuns. 'I'm not special, why would you be interested in me . . .?'"

Oft told is the ancient Arabian tale of the servant in Baghdad (probably best known as recounted in a play by W. Somerset Maugham, whose version is paraphrased here):

There was a merchant of Baghdad who sent his servant one morning to market, where the servant, buying provisions, was jostled by a woman in the crowd. The servant turned to see that it was Death who had jostled him, Death, in the disguise of a woman, looking directly into his eyes. Recoiling from a threatening gesture, the servant ran from the market, returned home pale and trembling, and reported to his master what had happened. The merchant loaned the servant his fastest horse, and the servant fled the city to escape his fate, racing to Samarra, where Death would be unable to find him. The merchant went down to the marketplace and found Death standing among the crowd. "Why did you make a threatening gesture to my servant when you saw him this morning?" the merchant wanted to know. To which Death replied: "That was not a threatening gesture. It was only a start of surprise. I was astonished to see him in Baghdad, for I had an appointment with him tonight in Samarra."

The belief that you can outlive your fate only as long as you can outrun it is your ever-present companion in the experience of survivor guilt. Like the servant, we all—Kevin, Brian, and I—had come upon Death in the marketplace. What made us different from the servant, of course, was that we knew how the story ended. Our escape was only temporary. All our running, we knew, was merely directed at our keeping that appointment in Samarra.

I spent the first week of my recovery at my parents' house outside Boston. Mary was still on the Cape and was more than qualified to look after me, but the house there, still under construction, wasn't quite ready to accommodate me. I wasn't yet up to roughing it. My sister Terry, still in her teens, was living at home with the folks, and she took responsibility for my physical therapy, which really consisted of my lying around thinking up clever ways to milk my injuries, at her expense and to her endless delight, and a lot of other clowning around.

"When you came home to recover," she recalls, "you were pretty upbeat, almost silly at times. I remember that you had lost a lot of weight. I had been handing my jeans down to you in those days, but they were now too big for you, which was a bit of a blow to my ego. You had a great sense of humor and a very positive attitude, two attributes the family employs when times get difficult. Humor, especially, has always worked as a great cover for all of us. I think we get funnier the more troubled we are."

Trouble didn't really reveal itself until later, once I was living on my own. Mary had returned to New York to start her new job—not until the fall, by which time I had advanced to the use of a cane, did I feel capable of negotiating the city—and I remained on the Cape with a lot of time to myself.

Says Terry, "I don't think you really crashed, so to speak, until after your physical recovery. There was a very dark period after you went back to the Cape. You became introspective and more distant. It seems to me that it was during this time that you really focused on the accident and how close you came to getting killed. This is the period of time where we were all acutely aware of how helpless we were in helping you through this process. We were all very worried about you. You and I would have long conversations into the night when I'd come to visit. But I can't say that any of it was helpful to you. We all just prayed that you'd survive it—though we had faith that you'd ultimately get through."

I did get through, ultimately, and my doing so justified my own faith in the attributes that had been engendered in me growing up.

"Once you figured things out—or decided that you would never have the answers you were seeking—you moved on," Terry says. "Your optimism and your confidence came back. And that's where I think the influence of the family comes in. Who you are was established long before the plane crash. It didn't change you. Who you were before was the person who was able to get through it. And it was the family that made you that way." It may be the military background, she says, but she believes that we as a family are not given to easy indulgence in a lot of existential thought. "We're not prone to drama. We don't dwell on things for too long. All setbacks are only temporary. You did the only thing you know how to do. You brushed yourself off and moved on."

As I look back on it now, I don't know how precisely to classify my correspondence with American Express, whether it was a latent example of the "signature silliness and humor" that Terry says she was alert to or an illustration of the short fuse on which I was operating at the time. It appears to be a little of both. When the charge for the flight showed up on my monthly statement, I dropped a note to the card company's Customer Service Department:

"I have paid, but dispute, the charge ... credited to Air New England. .... The flight on which the charged ticket was issued terminated short of its destination—the charge is subject to adjustment. Please contact the airline and credit my account accordingly."

I didn't ask for a refund, only that American Express pro-rate the charges, subtracting the cost of the last two and a half miles.

C arrying me out of the woods that night, the firemen, when-ever they paused to rest, would set down the backboard to which I was strapped and ask me how I was doing. The first time they asked, I told them, "I could use a cigarette."

One of them, suppressing a grin, advised me to quit smok-ing: "Hell, something like that could kill you," he said.

And we all broke out laughing. It was a welcome taste of the absurd.

Smoking is one of the bad choices I've made in my life. The quality of various other decisions, good or bad, is equally appar-ent. I don't give them too much thought. But there's one choice I made a long time ago whose consequences I continue to ques-tion, a decision the propriety of which still remained unresolved at the outset of my search: the decision I imposed upon my fel-low passengers to remove the injured girls from the airplane.

Did moving the girls injure them further?

The girls were not residents of the Cape, but their parents owned property here. And that property is still in the family. In Chatham, the town to which they were traveling that night, according to newspaper accounts of the crash, there is a phone listed under their name. It is a measure of Cape Cod's enchant-ment that while family members, with the passage of time, might have moved from their home in Michigan, their attach-ment to the Cape has remained constant.

Situated at the foggy elbow of the Cape, where the Atlantic meets Nantucket Sound, Chatham, distinctive for its extensive barrier beaches, gives its name to Chatham Light, a 2.8 million candlepower beacon that is visible twenty-five miles out to sea. Home to a commercial fish pier that is among the more vital in New England and to the Cape's most fertile shellfishery beyond the borders of Wellfleet, it is home to many people who work hard for a living, and its saloons pump plenty of workingman's beer. The slogan has since been co-opted by the residents of numerous other communities, but it was on the bumper sticker of a Chatham pickup where I first saw municipal pride expressed in the phrase "A quaint drinking village with a fishing problem." The million pounds of fish landed at the Chatham Pier in 2007 is probably a tenth of the catch landed there twenty years ago, but the longliners and draggers unloading there daily still constitute the town's most significant year-round industry.

Like a port of call for pirates or an open gold-rush town, Chatham is the town to which all the operators tended to gravitate back when you could identify a trawler captain by his Rolex, and it remains something of a rogue's paradise today. But that is not the image of Chatham promoted by the majority of residents who merely estivate there, showing up at the onset of summer, when, like coagulating algae, the population blooms from just under seven thousand to three times that. Chatham is a town of two minds about itself.

Fully half of the real property in Chatham consists of second homes. An upmarket resort that, to certain outsiders, is synonymous with Cape Cod—they may not really know the Cape, but yes, they've heard of Chatham—it is a town very special for its snob appeal. Its real estate is as expensive as that of any town on the Cape, but it's the only town where the summer people dress like the people on Nantucket. Nowhere off-island do you see so much of the pink they call Nantucket red. Every town on the peninsula has its souvenir T-shirts, but only Chatham does significant business in souvenir rugby shirts. This exaggerated peak-season sense of itself, as much as its concentration of year-round troublemakers, explains Chatham's reputation locally for the high quality of its cocaine.

The National Trust for Historic Preservation named Chatham to its 2007 list of America's Dozen Distinctive Destinations. Among the less class-conscious of its summer visitors is British prime minister Gordon Brown. The only Cape community other than Provincetown to support a commercial fishing fleet, it is the one Cape town, by contrast, that truly smacks of the idle rich. It reminds me a lot of Aspen, absent the latter's more obvious similarities to ancient Babylon.

My call to the Chatham phone number was the first I made in pursuit of the story after talking to Suzanne. Among the things I was surprised to learn from her was that she had seen the three Michigan sisters after the crash. She had been invited to visit the family in Chatham that summer after the last of the girls was released from the hospital. The visit, she told me, was brief, and her memory of it is vague, but as far as I was able to discover, it was one of only two occasions, both of them brief, on which survivors met after the crash.

The graciousness the parents had shown when they stopped by to thank me in the hospital was characteristic of their overall response to the tragedy. In a letter to the editor of the *Cape Cod Times* published four days after the crash, the girls' father expressed the family's gratitude to police, fire, and medical personnel and to the other passengers on the plane. A year later, in a phone call placed by a *Times* reporter doing follow-up on the anniversary of the crash, the girls' mother, speaking from

Michigan, said they were "all walking now and they're all going to school, but we still have concerns about their bone injuries. We're excited that they're alive and that we have our kids. Father's Day was very special here. Every day we're grateful that they're alive." The day the reporter called was the day the youngest started walking without crutches. "She threw away the crutches for the first time and is walking fine," her mother said. "But it will be a long time before she can run." Again praising the Cape's excellent community services, she told the reporter, "The support systems you have are fantastic. It made us feel very warm."

In anticipation of reaching out to the family, I looked forward to receiving an answer to the question that had troubled me for so long.

The season had come to an end on the Cape when I finally made the call. There were two listings under the name in Chatham. I remembered learning in the wake of the crash that the girls' parents had not been on-Cape when it happened but that someone else, perhaps a relative, had been waiting to meet the plane, and I was hoping, at most, when I put in the call, to get hold of an extended-family member who was a year-round Cape Cod resident, or, failing that, to pick up a recorded message directing me to a number in Michigan.

A woman answered the phone. When I explained who I was, she seemed confused and at the same time somewhat fascinated.

"I think you should talk to my husband," she said. She put him on the phone.

I gave the man my name, told him where I was calling from, and repeated what I'd told his wife: I said I'd survived a plane crash in 1979 with three sisters from Birmingham, Michigan, whose family I was trying to reach.

"I'm their father," he told me.

Presumably retired, clearly remarried, and evidently living year-round on the Cape, he wasn't actively impolite, but he wasn't cordial either. To give him a better fix on me, I reminded him of our meeting in the hospital, when he and his ex-wife had come by to thank me and return the shirt with which I'd covered their daughter.

"Yeah," he said, "I don't remember that."

I told him I was looking for help in reconstructing the events of that night.

"I'll have to get permission from them before I talk to you," he said. "If they're interested, they'll call you."

And he ended the conversation.

He called me himself a few days later.

"They don't want to participate," he announced.

Not cooperate. Participate. As if, rather than asking for help, I were offering his daughters a part in a movie.

It was hard to know how to respond. I'd talked to the fellow twice, now, for maybe a total of ninety seconds. In the face of such an abrupt refusal, one of the more natural follow-up questions is "Do you mind if I ask you why?" Sometimes the question is heartfelt. More often than not, it's a stupid question, an irrelevant one at best, a question reporters ask public officials to get them on the record, maybe get them to incriminate themselves further. Beyond that, the only purpose it serves is to keep people on the phone, give a caller time to explain himself and try to get a rhythm going. But asking why in this instance would have been disingenuous on my part, making me sound as insincere as he was trying to make me feel. It would have been disrespectful, not to him but to his daughters. Empathizing with my fellow survivors, I shared their disinclination. It was no easier for me than it was for his daughters to revisit the night in question.

All of this thinking was predicated, of course, on the assumption that he had asked their opinion, and I had to take him at his word.

"I understand how they feel," I told him.

Never in my life had I been more honest with an assertion. And I asked if it might be possible to get a few minutes of *his* time.

I really only asked him half of it. In the middle of that sentence, he hung up on me.

I was twenty-two years old, a freshly minted reporter in Washington. I had just been promoted from copyboy and put on general assignment. A couple of miles outside the city, in Prince Georges County, Maryland, a D.C.-bound Penn Central Metroliner, traveling 112 miles per hour, had struck a thirteen-year-old New Carrollton boy, dragging him over a mile and a half, and he had been declared dead on arrival at the hospital. My city editor handed the story to me.

"Give me two and a half takes," he said.

Two and a half pages, triple-spaced. A routine hard-news assignment.

I reported the story without leaving the desk, gathering the information over the phone. I typed it up, turned it in, and after it was marked up at the city desk, the story came back with a TK that hadn't been put there by me.

TK, appearing in copy, is editorial shorthand for "To Come," indicating information not yet available, maybe a fact on which a writer is waiting, or a statistic that, in the interest of efficiency and speed, he didn't stop to dig up. Its use is indispensable to a reporter. You write the story, you file the copy with the TK circled in pencil, and while the editor is making his cuts, you're on the phone to the cops, nailing down a description of the murder weapon, the one you described as "TK caliber."

But the TK added at the city desk was not inserted in the copy. Rather, it appeared in the margin, and it was preceded by the word "art," which in the newspaper business is how editors specify photography: Art TK.

"Nice job. Let's get a photo," my city editor told me.

A photo of the kid. The victim.

"OK."

But being new to the job, I wasn't sure where to begin.

"Talk to the family," he said.

The family. I'd managed to write the story without having to talk to members of the boy's family. The piece, as assigned, hadn't called for it. We were running it as a simple news item. That they'd talk to a reporter, of all people, in their hour of grief seemed unimaginable to me. I stepped away from the city desk thinking, *This isn't going to be fun*. I put it off for a little bit, didn't pick up the phone right away, and when I finally got around to making the call, the family didn't answer.

I remember it was late in the day. I think I might have called the boy's school, hoping to get a picture there. (It's possible I tried the school first in an effort to avoid calling the family.) Anyway, I came up short, and I tried calling the family again. Again no one picked up the phone, and there was no surer sign of my inexperience than the sense of relief I felt.

"I've been calling," I explained to my city editor. "I can't get an answer at the house."

He stared at me for a second. He nodded his head.

He said, "So get in your car."

"What do you want me to do?"

"I want you to get in your car, drive up there, knock on the door, and ask his parents for a picture."

"I don't think there's anyone home," I said.

"Be sure to stop by a phone," he said, "and call the desk before you come in."

It was dark when I arrived at the house. Lights were shining through all the windows. Cars were parked out front. There was no getting away from the reality that someone was going to answer the door. I rang the bell, and soon enough I was looking at the boy's father. I remember it all in black and white, like a scene out of classic film noir. There, alone on the lighted doorstep, I stood in my jacket and tie, sporting an open trench coat, a reporter now, doing my job, resigned to being greeted with all the disdain I believed my behavior deserved. Nothing about my being there was right. Nothing about it was appropriate. His grief was none of my business. And nonetheless, there I stood. I told him who I was.

He invited me in.

The door opened directly into the living room. Four or five people were sitting there, and most of them were crying. He ushered me into the kitchen, he and a young woman, a relative, who didn't seem much older than I; she was much too young, it seemed to me, to be in such firm possession of the poise and dignity she displayed. They asked me to sit. They offered me coffee. They may have offered me something to eat. I don't remember the details. All I remember, and will never forget, is how courteously I was received, how solicitous they were, how helpful. I remember a family utterly inconsolable going out of its way to make *me* feel comfortable.

We talked briefly, they gave me a photo, I thanked them, and they showed me out. The people in the living room were still crying when I left.

"We meet the worst people," a cop once told me, describing his job, "and the best people only at their worst."

I've been a reporter for most of my life, and I cannot understand why any of those people would agree to talk to the press. But experience has taught me that invariably they do. Their willingness to do so, story after story, has redounded to my benefit, yet even in the face of their willingness, I have never managed to escape a certain sense of discomfort with asking them to do it, especially in the kinds of circumstances I confronted that day in suburban Maryland. I'm uncomfortable by temperament with stealing people's privacy, however willing they might be to relinquish it. Some of my success as a writer, I think, results from that discomfort, which has pushed me out of necessity to seek alternative pathways into a story, avenues that circumvent the typical reporter's approach. Being a little bit thicker-skinned might make my job a little bit easier, but I don't think it would have taken me further. I've been merciless with my share of bureaucrats, politicians, and other all-weather stooges, but when dealing with humanity at large, I've discovered that there's very little takeaway value in coming on like Eyewitness News. The questions are all the same. The answers are all the same. That's why reporters ask them. And nothing newsworthy comes of it. Anyone with a response to personal tragedy that is in any way original—anyone with a genuinely interesting grasp on his or her innermost feelings on any subject—is going to volunteer it.

The response I received to my Chatham call was, to my mind, a reasonable one, the stance I would expect an intelligent person to take, the natural human default mode. What did the man have to gain by cooperating with me? He was protecting not simply his own privacy but, more important, that of his daughters. And more was at stake than their privacy. There were emotional consequences to consider, too. I think I might have responded differently on the other side of the request, had one of his daughters called seeking information from me, but that didn't enter my thinking then, and would not have changed my appraisal of things. He—and his daughters—had every right to decline.

He could have been nicer about it. He could have thanked me for understanding. He could have wished me well. He could have feigned a small measure of regret in consideration of the bond that his daughters and I shared. He could have said something about the weather. He didn't even give me a chance to say thank you. To apologize for any inconvenience I'd caused.

Of all the things he could have said, he had chosen instead to insult me. And rather than come away disappointed, I came away angry and offended. What upset me most was his dismissal, the peremptory nature of it, as if he were slamming the door on some parasitic segment producer looking to juice the boss's ratings. It was an implicit accusation of dishonesty against which I was unable to defend myself.

The disappointment alone was bad enough. It was early in my efforts to reach out to people, the second phone call I made. What if everyone reacted this way? Oddly, the fact that he was so impolite made the disappointment easier to take. I consoled myself with the understanding that, if what I needed was important enough, I could get it whether he liked it or not. What he refused to give I could take. I could show up at his door with notebook in hand and coerce his cooperation. I could implicitly threaten him with the possibility that I might make his not cooperating the story, that with absolutely no grounds to do so, I might wonder in print what the family was hiding. I could have acted the part of the stereotypical journalist.

Or I could honor the family's privacy.

The press in this country, however unworthy of its reputation for power, is something you challenge at your peril.

Reporters, for better or worse, swing significant weight. The better the reporter, the more judicious he is in throwing that weight around. My own take on the advantages the institution bestows is a product of the training I received, not only as a young reporter, but as the son of a naval officer and the graduate of a public high school that predates by almost a century and a half the Declaration of Independence, a school that educated, before educating me, five of the people who signed it. Not that you can't pick it up from a character like Spider-Man, but the sentiment is articulated best by Thucydides in his history of the Peloponnesian War, and it extends to my feelings about responsibility in general:

"Of all the manifestations of power, restraint impresses men most."

In the end I chose not to contact any of the sisters directly. I located their mother in Michigan, and on the off chance that her ex-husband hadn't talked to his daughters as he claimed, I wrote her a letter that explained what I was trying to do. I figured I owed the story that much.

Pressing survivors of the crash to open up to me in the face of an expressed unwillingness was a move I viewed as inherently self-defeating. In effect, it was telling them how to respond to the question I was out to explore, the answer to which was given to me by their very unwillingness to do so. It ill served the story I hoped to tell, both in its defiance of logic and in a narrative sense as well.

The third time I sat down with Suzanne, a year into our renewed acquaintance, I gave her the opportunity to explain her mother's comment that "The first two years were the worst," pushing the conversation in that direction without reference to the remark. And she answered just as she had the first time. She had put the crash behind her quickly, she said. And I was happy to leave it at that, appreciating that anything she might have told me in addressing the contradiction would have been anticlimactic to the contradiction itself. To my mind, what Mrs. Mourad had said was the better part of the story and the more telling part. And the same was true of the reaction I received from the father of the three sisters from Michigan. It revealed another, wholly individual response to the tragedy, which was illuminating on its own.

The family's business was no business of mine, a point reinforced by a conversation I had with Kevin Roberts shortly after reaching out to them. I told Kevin what I had run up against, and sharing my disappointment with him, I ventured my speculation on the reasons for the way I'd been treated.

"Looking back on something like that can't be easy for the parents," I told him. "The crash was probably more traumatic for them than it was for their kids."

Said Kevin, a father himself: "I guarantee you it was."

And for parents in those circumstances, he added, the post-traumatic stress lingers longer. Brian McCann, when I talked to him, said much the same thing, speaking specifically about his family, expressing his belief that what *could* have happened, the alternative prospect, is always a greater preoccupation for others than it is for the victims themselves.

Which may be worth considering in ultimately judging Mrs. Mourad's comment. It may more accurately reflect parental trauma than anything Suzanne experienced.

"Without my knowledge or my sister's," her brother, Pierre, told me, "my mom spoke with the dean of undergraduate housing at Rutgers, explained my sister's situation, explained that my presence in the dorm would be of great support to my sister, and [the dean] arranged for me to get into her dorm—all this without Sue or I knowing about it for some time."

Securing a dormitory room at Rutgers was typically quite hard, especially for a senior, which is what Pierre was at the time.

"I had wanted to stay in the dorms," he said, "so had applied as a matter of course, knowing it would be difficult. Neither Sue nor I knew that, after I applied, my mom intervened to ensure that I could get not only on-campus housing, but into the very [co-ed] dorm in which Sue resided."

Pierre, as part of a college exchange program, had spent his junior year at Oregon State, and he did not learn of the crash until he returned home that summer. "Given that I arrived on the scene a week after the accident," he said, "I was in the rather bizarre position of learning about that night and its aftermath sometimes years after the accident." Recalling that Suzanne, as she had told me herself, experienced trouble sleeping at night after the crash— as was true of most of the rest of us—he pointed to no other obvious difficulties but remembers being instructed by his mother "not to initiate conversations with my sister about the accident. I mostly hung out in the background as a quiet presence. It was a privilege for me to be able to help my sister, of course."

According to Jonathan Ealy, not only did the crash have an effect on him that was different from its effect on his parents, but the crash affects him now in a way that is different from the way it affected him then.

"Something I wouldn't have anticipated," he told me, "is that the emotions that go with it change over time. If you boil it down, it's a random thing that actually happened on a random night to a random group of people, and I was one of them and you were one of them, and when you're younger that's it, it's over on some level: 'Here's what happened, here's what it felt like, the truth is the truth and that's it.' It was just something else that happened. When you're young, things are just that literal. Over time, thinking about the same emotions and the same feelings . . . It's so easy to think about them completely differently with age. . . . Then I was a kid. I now have kids. It's the same way, I guess, as when you read a novel when you're eighteen and you read a novel when you're forty. It can mean a different thing to you."

The story of the air crash has changed not only in his reading of it but in his telling of it as well. In some ways, as with all such stories, it becomes easier to tell, he said. "It's almost like that grain of sand and there's been enough time to sort of gloss it over like a pearl and make it smooth." But the memories it conjures are complicated by the passage of time, and telling the story is made more difficult by the changes it must undergo. "It takes too long to tell as an adult."

The girls' mother never responded to my letter.

"You've got to be thinking, you've got to psyche yourself up for it. Otherwise you're going to get hit in the head," says former firefighter Bob Phillips, who was at home with his family that night when "they blew in a tone for the plane crash."

"It was a very long night," his wife, Paula, remembers.

And Phillips knew it was going to be long: "When you blow in all four stations . . ."

I found Bob Phillips on a warm July evening on the first-base side of Red Wilson Field at Dennis-Yarmouth Regional High School. He was sweating over the smoke of a large barbecue grill, wearing a long red apron and a conspicuous hat that on closer inspection revealed itself to be in the form of a cheeseburger. Of average height, blond, wearing distinctive half-glasses, Phillips was contributing his time to the Cape Cod Baseball League. He'd been volunteering for the past five or six years, working Yarmouth home games during the two-month season. Paula was pitching in at the nearby concession trailer.

It was the top of the eighth, the town's Red Sox were leading by six, the Backstop Grille was busy, and Phillips was going to be tied up for a while. Waiting for him to break free, I strolled over to stand by the visitors' dugout, and watched the Sox go on to win it against the Orleans Cardinals, 9–1.

The Cape League, established in 1885 and reorganized as the Cape Cod Baseball League in 1923, is America's premier amateur baseball league. The ten-team invitational league, playing a schedule that runs from mid-June to mid-August, is host to the nation's best college players. Fifteen percent of active players in Major League Baseball—about one in seven—are former Cape League players, and of active players who attended four-year colleges, more than one in every three played baseball here. Some two hundred former Cape League players are currently playing in the majors, and more than a thousand play in professional baseball overall.

Athletes invited to play in the league are housed by local families, and many work part-time to pay for their room and board, seeking jobs in the community, as do most college students who spend their summers on the Cape. New Mexico governor and former presidential candidate Bill Richardson worked as a landscaper the summer he pitched for Cotuit. The University of Hartford's Jeff Bagwell, who worked for the prevailing wage at the local Friendly's restaurant when he played for the Chatham Athletics, signed a $96 million contract extension with the Houston Astros in 2001. But one need not look back even that far for an indication of the talent on view at the typical Cape League game. Jacoby Ellsbury, a student at Oregon State University, played for Falmouth in 2004. In the 2007 World Series, he started at center field for the Boston Red Sox, batting an extraordinary .438—the best among starters for either team—in their four-game sweep of the Colorado Rockies.

Ballplayers and their host families maintain contact over the years, and the continuity of those relationships makes for a special link between Cape Cod and the national pastime. The league serves as something of a hatchery for Major League Baseball, which has provided financial support since the 1960s. It is where young hitters swing wooden bats for the first time and where young pitchers start learning how to break them. It also allows for character screening before admission to the Show: *He lived with upstanding citizens for a couple of months, he didn't drink, he didn't get high, he didn't rape anybody— yeah, our money's safe, we can sign him.* So professional has the process become that the athletes today, like Olympians in the former Soviet Union, rather than shucking clams and mowing lawns to earn their keep, will more often be found conducting youth baseball clinics, providing instruction to local kids whose parents sign them up either to learn the game or advance their skills.

Like the seashore itself, the league is one of Cape Cod's unmatched treasures. There is no better place in the country to watch a baseball game than the terraced bank of grass that rises from the edge of the diamond at Eldredge Park in Orleans, the home field of the Lower Cape's Cardinals. There, on a warm night, a few blocks from the ocean, you can nestle in beside the base path and cheer for future major-league all-stars—Barry Zito, Frank Thomas, Nomar Garciaparra, Mark Teixeira, Darin Erstad, Mike Lowell, just to name a few of those who are currently playing in the bigs—even talk with them if you want, *during* the game. And the baseball is free of charge.

So are the services of supporters like Bob Phillips, the man I was in Yarmouth to see. Phillips, fifty-five, an electronics technician, is employed by a local alarm company. He has been installing and servicing security systems for almost twenty years. For a dozen years before that, he worked for Datamarine International. For thirty years, while working full-time, he indulged what he referred to as a hobby, one for which he was paid on an as-needed basis, serving as a call firefighter in Yarmouth. He retired as a captain in 2005.

Among the numerous personnel who had put in duty the

night of the plane crash—career, call, and volunteer personnel from Yarmouth and surrounding towns—Phillips had been
singled out to me as having something more to offer than the
others. For twenty years, on top of all his additional activities,
he had been donating time to the Boy Scouts. He was currently
a unit commissioner for Boy Scout Troop 50 in Yarmouth Port.
Phillips was the only firefighter for whom the camp surrounding the site of the crash existed as anything more than a memory. The camp remained unvisited by all the others to whom
I had talked; to them it was still and would always be a vast,
inhospitable wilderness known only for the horrific rescue that
had taken them there that night. To Phillips it was familiar territory, terrain he had covered since then and continued to cover
in his work with the scouts. Any confusion I might have had
about the wreck's location he would be in a position to correct.

We talked about it briefly. He corroborated what I'd been
told. He alerted me to certain clues that existed in an area called
Prospect Hill. When we finished with that, I showed him the
photograph I'd shown William Smith, the picture of the unidentified paramedic checking me for injuries as I lay in the woods.
I'd shown it to all the firefighters I'd managed to speak to, and
so far nobody's guess as to his identity had proved accurate.
Phillips wasn't able to help me there either, and with what I was
learning about the deployment in question, I wasn't surprised.

At one point, according to the crash report, the Yarmouth
Fire Department had forty-eight of its sixty-five-man firefight-
ing force involved in the emergency. (Some fifty people, it was
estimated, not all of them firefighters, were involved in the
search itself.) And mutual aid was substantial. Fire depart-
ments from Hyannis, Dennis, Harwich, Barnstable, and West
Barnstable provided fifteen additional men, and each department provided an ambulance.

"We needed the buses," Phillips explained.

Yarmouth had only two.

We sat at a picnic table, talking, while Philips had something to eat. Fans were making their way to the parking lot. The sun was getting ready to set.

"The mosquitoes were hungry," Phillips said, casting his thoughts back to the night of the search.

The mosquitoes and the gnats, feeding in swarms, closed in on the firefighters as they bushwhacked their way through the forest. All the firefighters I talked to mentioned it when they looked back on that night. They remembered it without my asking. For me and the other survivors, bugs were not a significant problem, not that any of us is able to recall. Maybe it was the absence of light. We lay in elemental, uncontaminated darkness, far from any source of illumination for the insects to home in on. Maybe the kerosene in which we were soaked acted as a repellant. Maybe it's just that we remember other things more.

Phillips, like other members of the search party, described what he found at the scene from a circumscribed point of view, a perspective that was necessarily limited by the professional demands of the emergency.

"You didn't wander much," he said.

No firefighter working the crash site focused on more than one victim. I'd picked up on this fact while talking to Smith and Pete Norgeot, too. On the typical rescue, Phillips said, four men would usually be enough to carry a single stretcher. But evacuating the injured over the distance and terrain that he and the others faced on the night of the crash would call on the efforts of more. Once a firefighter arrived at the scene, his work was pretty much cut out for him.

"You started collecting people and keeping them."

Phillips was one of "six or seven," not counting the paramedic, who carried the eighteen-year-old sister out of the woods.

I did not ask him to describe her injuries and would not have expected him to share such information even if it were something he could recall. I explained to him that I had not talked to any of the sisters. I mentioned my call to Chatham.

He had a Chatham story, too.

Sometime in the early to mid nineties, he told me, he was doing annual off-season maintenance there on a residential alarm system his company had installed. He had serviced the account before, he said, and just as had happened on the previous visits, the name on the account struck him as familiar.

"The name bugged me. It stuck in my head. And I couldn't understand why."

On this call, his third, he caught up with the caretaker of the unoccupied house.

"Where are these people from?" he asked.

"Michigan," the caretaker replied.

It was the caretaker, not a relative, who'd been waiting for the girls at the airport. And this was still their house. Phillips told me that he and the caretaker talked for a couple of hours. Some fifteen years had passed since he had entered the woods looking for the girls. The three were grown women now.

"One's a lawyer," Phillips told me. "One went into emergency medicine."

"She's an MD," I said, "a radiologist."

I told him where she worked.

"Women are always harder," I said, "they get married and change their names."

But locating them had been easy enough.

Phillips told me that the Yarmouth Firefighters and Relief

Association had taken a special interest in the girls, delivering gifts to them when they were hospitalized.

"We were sending stuff up," he said, "on a fairly regular basis."

It was not unusual for firemen, especially in the summer, he said, to be in and out of the hospital three or four times a day, and the local fire-and-rescue guys would stop between emergency runs, checking with the nurses they knew to see how the girls were doing.

Later, when I talked to Robert Jenney, the Yarmouth EMT who the night of the crash had argued outside the hospital with the Channel 5 reporter, he told me that the plight of the youngest sister was "the thing that got me most." With her parents in Michigan when it happened, he said, "she had nobody," and the firefighters responded to that. "Kids affect you more than anybody else. The guys fell in love with the little girl, and some of them stopped by to visit her."

None of the firefighters I talked to was sufficiently familiar with the girls' medical conditions to tell me whether moving them had somehow made their condition worse.

Phillips and I talked until just before darkness set in.

"It's getting late," Paula reminded her husband.

Everybody had left the ballpark, and it was time for him to go. If he had been home since leaving for work that day, it had been for only a few minutes. And whether baseball, the Boy Scouts, or something else, probably sooner rather than later, he would be volunteering more of his time. First, he'd be reporting to work, he told me, just as he had done after answering the call for the air crash twenty-eight years earlier. After spending all night in the woods, giving time to the one hobby for which he was paid, Phillips that Monday morning—to the astonishment of an employer who when Phillips walked in was following breaking news of the rescue—showed up at work on time.

Leaving the ballpark, walking to my car, thinking about what Phillips had told me, I had come as close as I was going to get to knowing what had become of the three sisters in whose fate I had intervened when they and I were a lot younger. I would never know the extent of the injuries they suffered or the extent to which their injuries might have been attributable to me.

I never did find the paramedic who treated me. But I have little doubt that, had I been able to identify him, I'd have found him pretty close at hand.

"People on the Cape," says Mary Ellen, who still works as a nurse at the hospital, "they really don't go very far."

If this story has taught me anything, it certainly has taught me that. The circles here, when they close, turn in on themselves rather neatly, and often no farther away than the white pages. There I found the name of the copilot, or someone who shares his name. I wanted to believe it was he, and I had every reason to think so. At the time of the crash, he was identified as a resident of Vermont who had been with Air New England for only two months, but he was also said to have a local connection; he was the nephew of a selectman in the town of Sandwich. The story that the *Cape Cod Times* ran on the anniversary of the event reported that he was "flying again for Air New England," and if what Suzanne had been told was true, he'd had even more cause than that to take up permanent residence on the Cape. When Suzanne walked into the airport that night, she noticed, amid the chaos, an airline employee, a ticket agent in the office behind the counter, sobbing. This distraught young woman, she was later told, was the copilot's fiancée.

"He was a really aggressive guy," said Jonathan Ealy. "Helping him was sort of an odd thing . . . an odd combination of his being authoritative and emergency trained and sort of bossing me around, and his really hurting, really being in pain. At the beginning we were talking, he was lucid. By the end I was just trying to keep him awake, just making him respond to things and give me signals. His breathing was shallow, he was less lucid, he kind of got worse and worse, and I was talking to him, I was telling him stories and I was doing the freshman psychology self-hypnosis: 'OK, we're on a beach . . .' And for ten or fifteen minutes I went into shock, I got real faint and I started shaking, and then I came back out of it again. I was hurting like hell after an hour and a half, and he was just in terrible pain, and I'm like, 'Oh, don't die on me. . . .' He was having trouble breathing. I was contemplating helping him breathe and that was not my first choice of things to do. . . . The last half hour he was not with me."

The copilot and I had never laid eyes on each other. To me he was just the memory of a voice in the fog, and his recollection of me had to be that much cloudier, if he remembered much about me at all. He would have had no way of knowing, as we shouted to each other in the night, which of the male passengers he was talking to. The exchange was brief and unpleasant. Our association didn't begin on very good terms. I would add that neither did it end that way, but in pondering the prospect of calling him—him, for some reason, more than the others—I realized that it didn't end at all. Our association was permanent. And if we never met each other again, that wouldn't change.

Memories and what we do with those memories, how they are physiologically encoded, inform an expanding branch of neuroscience, Elissa Koff tells me. Dr. Koff is the Margaret Hamm Professor of Psychology Emerita at Wellesley College, but to me she has always been, well, just Elissa. We have been acquainted for some thirty years now, and not until recently, when I explained to her what I was up to, did I have more than a vague idea of what she did for a living or how distinguished she was academically. In the Cape Cod equivalent of an over-the-back-fence conversation one summer evening, she and her husband, Ray, a physician, saved me hours of library research.

Traumatic events, "highly salient emotional events," she tells me, are encoded differently from other events. They are processed by the autobiographical memory in a way that makes them unforgettable—literally. She explains the phenomenon as an evolutionary mechanism for survival. She offers the rudimentary example of a primitive human, availing himself of a particular watering hole, losing an appendage to the jaws of a predator—and remembering not to go back. Such memories are indelible, she says, inescapable "on a neurophysiological level," because they are something you *must* remember in order to survive. The evolutionary viability of the species depends on the permanent processing of traumatic memories. We are supposed to remember bad things forever. It is how our brains are wired.

As a way of understanding posttraumatic stress disorder, the Koffs directed me to the work of neurobiologist James L. McGaugh of the University of California at Irvine, a pioneering researcher into the biochemical link between emotion and memory. According to McGaugh, it is the release of the stress hormones adrenaline and cortisol, triggering the release of another hormone, norepinephrine, that reinforces the permanence of traumatic memories. He says that while the mechanism has only recently been the subject of scientific inquiry—he himself has been investigating it for about half a century—its effects have long been known.

In the past, he writes in his 2003 book *Memory and Emotion*, "before writing was used to keep historical records, other means had to be found to maintain records of important events. . . . To accomplish this, a young child about seven years old was selected, instructed to observe the proceedings carefully, and then thrown into a river. In this way, it was said, the memory of the event would be impressed on the child and the record of the event maintained for the child's lifetime."

Roger Pitman, who views McGaugh as "the leading behavioral neuroscientist of our time," is a professor of psychiatry at Harvard Medical School whose work on understanding PTSD the Koffs also commended to my attention. Pitman believes the disorder reinforces itself. "In the aftermath of a traumatic event," he has said, "you tend to think more about it, and the more you think about it, the more likely you are to release further stress hormones, and the more likely they are to act to make the memory of that event even stronger."

The plane crash is a textbook example of the traumatic events Pitman talks about, the salient emotional events Elissa Koff, citing the work of McGaugh, says you must remember to ensure your survival. For everyone who lived through it—the copilot, my fellow passengers, and me—the memory of that night is inerasable. Hence the permanence of our association, even if fate, or I, were never again to bring us together. All of us, as a result of our shared experience, are heirs to a common destiny. At those times when remembrance of the past imposes itself on the present, it is we, as ghosts on the periphery, who haunt one another's dreams.

Understanding this, I understood why, when sitting with Suzanne in that first hour of our reacquaintance, I felt as though she and I had known each other all our lives. It was a feeling that also expressed itself in my meetings with the others. The connection we shared had some of the outward qualities of the bond that exists between siblings, observable in, if not measured by, the things that are left unspoken.

"You share something with these people that no one else shares with them. You share something very deep together," Richard Morrill told me.

I'd known Dick Morrill for years in a kind of run-into-him-around-town kind of way. I wouldn't have said we were pals—I was much better acquainted with his brother—but I'd certainly spent enough time with him and talked to him often enough to like him.

Recently I got to know him a lot better.

Not only is Morrill bright, he has terrific performance skills. He knows how to command an audience. He is one of those guys who smiles when he talks, not like you and me, but like Harold Hill in *The Music Man,* albeit with much more sincerity, one of those engaging, outgoing characters who talk and smile at the same time. He can converse intelligently on a range of subjects. There isn't a lot you can't talk to him about, but it's always more fun to listen, and he is remarkably forthcoming with information about himself. And so it came as something of a surprise when, after knowing him for so many years, I learned how much about him I really didn't know.

"Have you talked to Dick Morrill yet?" a friend of mine inquired, when I explained that I was doing research on post-traumatic stress.

"Why would I talk to Dick?"

"He's studied it pretty thoroughly. He can probably direct you to the right sources."

I knew Dick Morrill as a carpenter. I wasn't familiar with his educational background. Out here, at the end of the Cape, you stop asking questions about things like that after you run into your third or fourth Fulbright scholar with a commercial fishing license, your second or third career bartender with a background on Wall Street. These are the escapees I mentioned earlier—I can introduce you to an Eastham stonemason who can translate Virgil without breaking a sweat—the people I like to think of as refugees, men and women who visited the Outer Cape and decided they wanted to stay, learning to do, as Morrill himself would tell me later, "whatever they could that would allow them to make a living here," learning in his case "to be a carpenter . . . and an innkeeper . . . and a musician . . . and an actor." They show up here from all over the country, trading in their career goals for—and they all use the same expression—"quality of life," which means that, more than punching a clock, they like living on Jimmy Buffet time. That's the secret of life on the Outer Cape: Nobody has any money, and we're all living as though we've got trust funds.

Morrill could easily have been an academic in an earlier life, a psychology professor like Elissa Koff. He was clearly a studious fellow, and he certainly had the visual attributes of at least one notable scholar. Lean and bespectacled, ranging over six foot three and exhibiting the excellent, upright posture that teachers and parents encourage, he brought to mind, somewhat vaguely and minus the lugubrious trappings, the classic renderings of the schoolmaster Ichabod Crane in "The Legend of Sleepy Hollow."

The first time I saw him, I was new to the Cape, and he was rising to address the town meeting, calling for a vote to direct the federal government to recognize the community as a nuclear-free zone. "As I remember, some other people wrote it and asked me to stand up and make the motion," he told me, when I reminded him of it recently. "It must have passed, since there is not one single nuclear weapon in our town."

Before calling him, I asked my friend where it was that Morrill came by his expertise.

"It's something Dick's been into forever," he told me.

Well, not quite forever, I discovered, but at least since 1968.

In 1968, Dick Morrill was twenty-seven years old, living in Saigon, and working as a flight mechanic for Air America, the civilian airline owned and operated by the Central Intelligence Agency that supported covert military operations in Southeast Asia.

"We did stuff the military couldn't do," Morrill told me, when he and I sat down to talk. "As far as we were concerned, there were no rules. Our motto was Anything, Anytime, Anywhere."

In June of that year, the year of the Tet offensive, he was aboard a helicopter training flight with an instructor pilot and two first officers being checked out for promotion to captain, one of whom was sitting with him in the back of a Bell 204B, known in its military configuration as the UH-1 Iroquois, and more famously by its GI nickname, the Huey. They were practicing emergency landings between Saigon and Long Binh, "not an area where, if you went down, they'd come and shoot you," Morrill said, so there was no fear of that when the helicopter crashed.

Morrill isn't an academic. He is a graduate of the school of horrible experience.

"It was really flaring . . . knees up . . . the tail rotor was hitting . . . at sixty miles per hour, it took only about eight seconds . . . the chopper flipped . . . *No, no, no, no!* . . ." The helicopter went into a skid. "*No, this can't happen . . . I don't want to die . . .*" pinning him facedown beneath it.

"I automatically went into prayer. . . ."

There was no pain, he said, but there was terror.

"I knew I was gonna die, I knew it was gonna explode. . . ."

He knew the fuel in the line would keep the machine running for three minutes, and he kept yelling instructions on how to shut the engine down, screaming out the location of the emergency fire handle to his fellow crew members. Only two of them were alive, and the one who was conscious was in far worse condition than Morrill.

"I was trapped, and I was pissed. I was so pissed at God. . . ."

What if it's not Jesus? What if it's Buddha? Morrill found himself wondering, excited in a strange way that he was now about to learn the answer. All the while shouting instructions.

The engine quit after three minutes, and he remained pinned for another twenty, until he finally heard the voices of the U.S. military patrol that saved him.

His posttraumatic stress was severe. "For a year, I could never be alone," he told me. "I could never be above the fourth floor in a building." It stayed with him, in one form or another, for twenty-eight years.

"Whenever I talked about the crash, I could feel tension," he said. "I spoke in a way that was different. It takes energy to suppress these things." In an innovative acupressure procedure, he found a trauma therapy that finally cured him.

A final word about memory and emotion:

Memories laid down in detail during significant emotional events have a vivid, photographic quality that has led psychologists to coin the term *flashbulb memory*. Every memory is slightly altered every time you retrieve and refile it; not only are you calling up the original memory, but you are also calling up the last time you remembered it. The difference between normal memory and flashbulb memory is not accuracy, but *perceived* accuracy. People *believe* their flashbulb memories to be more accurately and vividly laid down.

"They're vivid," says Elissa Koff, "but not necessarily accurate. The information you put in is not the same as you pull out."

My memory of the crash is of coming around kneeling on the deck with the seat strapped to my back. I also remember, immediately after the crash, describing it that way to others: the seat coming forward with me, ripping free of the fuselage. According to the NTSB report, "The seat in position 1A [that of the eldest sister] was separated from its aft floor and wall attachments when trees penetrated the area," a failure due to impact damage. "The tie-down chain ... was actually severed at only one seat location due to decelerative forces," and that was where Suzanne had been sitting. "Seat unit 4BC was found collapsed on the floor," its anchor bolts "sheared in a forward-inboard position."

In the report, no mention is made of my seat collapsing. I asked Suzanne what she remembered. She told me her seat "collapsed into the seat in front of it. . . . When I stood up, you were still in your seat . . . I do not remember you being on the floor."

Scientists who study memory will tell you, as Dr. Koff explained the paradox to me, "The safest, purest memory is the memory that's never retrieved."

I didn't talk to the copilot after our brief exchange of words that night, after our shouting at each other in the darkness as we were evacuating the airplane. I caught a glimpse of him in the hospital, but only fleetingly, a few days later. We passed each other on gurneys as I was being wheeled out of X-ray after my surgical consult. I can't explain how I knew it was he. I saw only the top of his head, and I would not have recognized his face had I seen it.

His testimony before the NTSB was corroborated by that of others, and he was exonerated by the board. I don't know if I saw the transcript of his testimony, and thus I cannot explain why, but my tendency had always been to ascribe to him a palpable measure of bitterness, a rancor unalleviated by time. That may have been a mistake, an insinuation of the anger I witnessed that night—anger I shared—into something I read much later.

The one time he and I had talked to each other, he was disgorging blood and slipping into clinical shock. I was looking for leadership, calling out to him in the dark, only to learn I was on my own. I'll never forget what he said or the chill that came over me when he said it.

He shouted, "Copilot's doing his job!"

An awful emptiness rose in my stomach, an emptiness that revisits at night when I hear him say it in my sleep.

While there is no upside to victimization, there is a certain purity in the victimization that comes with surviving a plane wreck, for it is unclouded by any suggestion of contributory negligence. It's not like crashing your car. A plane crash survivor is never troubled by questions of what he might have done to avoid or prevent it. Unless, of course, he is a member of the crew. The airplane's first officer did not benefit from that purity, and it is not hard to believe that he struggled for months, as the investigation of the crash dragged on, with the simultaneous challenges of asking himself those troubling questions while defending himself against blame for errors that were not his.

"Apart from [his] being horribly wounded, I got the feeling he was fighting his own internal sense of, Oh, my God, I'm the copilot . . . wrestling with trying to get through the emotional side of accepting the fact that he'd just crashed his airplane. . . . There was a lot of talk about 'This wasn't my fault. . . .' "

Jonathan Ealy, not because of anything that transpired after the crash, but because of the view he'd had into the cockpit from where he was sitting before it happened, was called to testify at the two-day NTSB hearing held in Cambridge in mid-September:

"Remember when Sears used to sell the double-knit suits

where you could reverse the pants and the jacket and make it real sporty . . . ? Yeah, I had to get the chocolate brown double-knit three-piece. . . . I got done testifying, and I think it was the second hearing I testified at, and a big guy on crutches came up," introduced himself by name, "and said, 'Can I buy you a roast beef sandwich?' I don't think we ended up going to lunch, I think I had to [get back to campus]. But I got to see him. And after all the unreality of testifying, that was sort of like a real . . . Oh, yeah, there really *is* a guy, it really *did* happen."

It was the last time he saw the man whose life he had saved, but not the last time he heard of him.

"Alaska's full of pilots, and one of the bars I liked to go to was full of pilots," he told me. One night with a friend who knew them, he found himself drinking with a group of pilots who worked with the copilot at Delta Airlines. "He flew for Delta apparently. That was back in ninety-four or ninety-five. They knew him real well and had heard about the plane crash and had heard about me."

Aviators belong to a community in which scuttlebutt is highly valued, and in the conversation Jon had with the Delta pilots fifteen years after the crash, they alluded to circumstances only speculated on at the time of the accident. The fact that the underlying information might have been provided to them by the copilot makes their remarks worth considering.

In their understanding, Air New England at the time of the crash had been the target of a job action, afflicted by an outbreak of what they referred to as "pilot flu," a work slow-down in which numerous pilots had collectively called in sick. Alleged at the time, but not pursued by the press, it was why Parmenter had been assigned to fly.

Parmenter's recent flying time, his actual time in the air, according to the accident report, "had been limited to 12 hours in the last 90 days" leading up to the day of the crash. He had flown most of that time in clear weather, and it was possible, said the NTSB, "that the captain's proficiency, particularly in instrument meteorological conditions, was degraded by the lack of recent experience."

The pilots, in discussing the crash with Jon, described the airplane's steep descent as intentional. Parmenter, they said, was going for what is known as a "hot look," dropping below the cloud cover, attempting, in the words of the NTSB, which considered the possibility, "to visually acquire a familiar landmark, the ground or the landing lights." A willful breaking of the minimum altitude restriction, the maneuver was an unsafe violation of FAA regulations, and testimony revealed that Parmenter had used similar "duck under" procedures on other flights. On one such flight his copilot, a qualified captain, took control of the aircraft from him at six hundred feet, and leveled out at two hundred. In the case of his fatal crash, however, the NTSB concluded, it was more probable that the descent was unintentional.

Had Parmenter's descent been intentional, and had the copilot been aware of it, there would have been little the copilot could have done about it. Crew coordination procedures, since then, have tightened up considerably, but in the culture that prevailed at the time, no matter how immature or irresponsible his behavior, when a captain said, "I've got the airplane," he had the airplane. Overriding the legendary Parmenter would have taken a lot more authority than that possessed by a probationary junior employee whose representation by the pilots' union was still eight months away.

"I can tell you from the pilots that I met in that bar," Jonathan Ealy said, "that would be [his] story, that Parmenter had been there forever, that he was the new kid, and he didn't have any authority to tell the guy what to do."

And though not without justification, it seemed as if it were something he was still angry about fifteen years later.

I'd like to say my own anger passed quickly.

"In the hospital you were mad," says my sister Elaine. Mad enough that she remembers it almost thirty years later. "Anger is a good response."

There are two kinds of anger at issue, however. What Elaine witnessed in the immediate aftermath of the crash, simmering beneath the surface but not invisible to my family, was the initial eruption of anger that saved my life or might have, had the plane been engulfed by fire. No doubt exacerbated by a frustration with my physical injuries, it is the same anger one shows right after taking a punch, and she viewed it in a positive light as an alternative to fear or sadness, preferable to what she describes as the "poor me" posture of the victim.

"I think it's healthier to get mad," she says. "It puts you in a stronger position."

A stronger position from which to counterpunch.

It's the kind of anger perhaps best explained with the help of a vocabulary a little bit broader than that which my sister characteristically exhibits, the kind of vocabulary I tend to exhibit on a pretty regular basis: I wasn't angry, I was pissed off.

But there is another kind of anger at play, anger over the longer term.

Dick Morrill, who remembers being enraged when pinned beneath his helicopter, agrees that anger is a natural reaction but also understands the consequences of failing to get beyond it. "Anger," he told me, "is like taking poison and hoping the other guy gets sick."

The best I can claim is that I was quick to overcome the

anger I was able to identify. The anger I focused on the pilot, for example, I transcended almost immediately. Early in my recuperation, I realized there was no percentage in holding that kind of grudge.

The equanimity I achieved is reflected in Suzanne's experience, in the memory of a chance encounter she shared with me when she and I first talked. Twenty years had passed since the crash, and Suzanne was visiting the Cape Cod Museum of Natural History, a modest, much cherished enterprise here, in Brewster, an institution staffed in large part by elderly volunteers. On the name tag of the woman ringing her up at the gift counter, she recognized a familiar surname. Without much thought, she asked the woman, "Are you any relation to George Parmenter?"

The room went silent, she told me.

"He was my husband," Doris Parmenter replied.

Suzanne, introducing herself, explained to the pilot's widow who she was.

"I know who you are," Mrs. Parmenter said.

And now, of course, Suzanne was asking herself, *Where did I think this conversation was going to go?* Breaking the uncomfortable silence, she said the only thing that made any sense, closing the painful interchange with the one thing that served to say it all.

"It was a long time ago," she said.

I suppose I could come up with a variety of reasons for choosing not to call Mrs. Parmenter, which is a choice I made early on. Not the least of them was imagining her heartbreak at the sound of my voice when I told her why I was calling. The simplest explanation is that I just saw nothing to be gained by it. Suzanne's story merely reaffirmed a decision I'd already arrived at by instinct.

The anger I shook off shortly after the crash was easy enough to shed. But Mary believes there was a deeper anger that took me longer to get beyond. I defer to her judgment as that of a person who was in a position to know. If she's right, the anger was so unfocused as to be invisible to me.

"You changed completely after the crash," she said, "that summer on the Cape. I think it changed you forever."

But she admits that the impact was difficult to measure. "There were so many other changes, so many other things going on, all of which you had no control over," the most obvious being sudden success. "There's never been anything linear about your life," she said, the word echoing Elaine's reference to an absence of continuity.

Mary and I split up the following summer and remained separated for more than a year. Among the people I met that year was an aspiring writer, Bo Bryan, who has remained a friend ever since. I met him through my friend and colleague Maryanne Vollers, who at the time, before distinguishing herself as the gifted author she is today, was an editor at *Rolling Stone*. Recently I talked to Bo, who would have been insensitive to any changes in me resulting from the crash, not having known me before the changes took place. But he was sensitive to other things, anger being one of them.

"One of the first things Maryanne told me about you before we met," he said, "was the story of your crash and the interruption of your career. Whether you knew it or not, and I suspect you had no idea, the event pervaded the atmosphere around you, the sort of David and Goliath nature of it, Goliath being the force of gravity as it collapsed for a while your ability to go on writing big books. . . . I wondered back then if, while you were laid up, you felt any bitterness . . . while you couldn't work, couldn't produce the follow-up bestseller."

Whatever bitterness I might have harbored at the time did not manifest itself in a way that was identifiable to Bo, who said he remembered my being somewhat subdued, a little less frenetic than the people around me.

"Later I understood," he said, "that your body had taken a tremendous beating. None of us who were close to you then knew what it was like to be physically limited in ways that weren't going to change. You had been given an advance look into the stage of life that we're all much closer to now."

In the course of that second summer, another lifelong friend I made was Gregory Katz, a reporter for the *Cape Cod Times*. Greg was the writer who, on the anniversary of the crash, wrote the piece for the *Times* on how the survivors were faring, the article in which the mother of the three Michigan sisters was quoted, though he and I had met before that. Today, having since won a Pulitzer Prize for international reporting, he is an overseas correspondent with the Associated Press. He doesn't recall my being entirely subdued.

"I remember you being in serious physical pain and having your physical ability to write hampered to a great degree," he told me recently, "and my feeling is that you actually turned away from writing at this point in favor of celebrity. The crash made it impossible for you to write and gave you lots of empty time to fill up. You filled the time kind of coasting on your fame as long as you could."

He described it as "a destructive time."

Admittedly, with the exception of money, which after the crash was in short supply and would continue to be for the next couple of years—affirming my status as only half famous—I didn't lack for any of those kinds of things in which celebrities indulge when they have nothing better to do with their time, those kinds of things that go from self-indulgent to self-destructive when the same people have nothing better to do with their lives. There was no shortage of female companionship, no deficiency in the brand of refreshment that in another age, in a lost-weekend kind of way, would have been provided by whiskey. All that, and rock and roll, too. But how much of this behavior was attributable to the crash rather than merely exaggerated by it is open to question. It wasn't as if I had been driving under the limit up to then; what happened was a little bit more like pulling the speed governor off a racecar.

This is the "very dark period" that Terry was calling attention to.

"Maybe the whole thing had something to do with testing your indestructibility," she said. " 'If the plane crash didn't kill me, nothing will.' "

That, of course, is indisputable. Daredevil behavior in the aftermath of escaping death is something of a cliché. My own behavior along those lines, even at its most memorable, was nonetheless pretty lame. I never had the courage to really push the envelope. And I'd describe my response as situational rather than symptomatic. But I remember certain moments, alone on the Cape that year after everyone had returned to the world, finding myself behind the wheel and thinking exactly what Terry described. I remember speeding along the deserted straightaway that parallels the ocean, double-clutching through the twisting roads that wind through the woods of the national park, the radio speakers cranked to the point where I could actually feel the music—tunes about to go platinum recorded by people I knew personally but hadn't seen in a while—thinking, "I'm wearing my seat belt. If I hit something, how bad can it be?"

But my friends and family saw more in this unhealthy behavior than I did, and they see more in it today than I can, looking back. If I seem to be cavalier about it, if I seem insufficiently penitent or (probably more damning in such exercises as these) inadequately flagellant—if I don't twelve-step you here, if I appear to be "in denial"—it's because I come at the subject from an entirely different frame of reference.

Not only did I write one of the more famous books on dangerous behavior, but as a consequence, I've made the intimate acquaintance of a lot of those kinds of people who give the concept new meaning. I've witnessed it as practiced by the world's most serious professionals. I've watched the play-offs. And believe me, I don't qualify. I'm talking about self-destructive behavior that comes with the warning "Don't try this at home." These are characters who will tell you that your best measure of whether the wheels have really come off the bus is the number of parties you've thrown at which you were the only guest.

Look for evidence where you want. What my friends, my loved ones, and my family are reluctant to mention is that, like a lot of people a lot of the time, I can simply be a fool, and for a while there, back then—and I won't argue with them about the reasons—I was a bigger fool than usual.

I called the number I had for the copilot several times and received no answer. I left voice-mail messages twice. I placed the calls at various times of the day, all of which were met by a variety of theatrical outgoing messages recorded by the woman of the house. The listing in the local phone book showed the copilot, if it were he, to be married to a woman named Priscilla. I presumed it was she whose voice I was becoming familiar with. I don't know why she didn't return my calls. It was possible, I suppose, that she lived in the house alone. Maybe I had the wrong number. I wondered, and will continue to wonder, if she was the ticket agent who had been weeping that night.

F our days after the crash—some eighty-eight hours and thirty-three minutes from the moment that plane hit the trees—I celebrated my thirty-third birthday. I don't have the actuarial figures on males of my generation; I'd like to think it's possible I'll live longer than sixty-six years, but however long I live or don't, that moment will always be halftime. Everything up to and everything following will always be before and after. While whatever it cost or contributed may or may not be obvious, or may simply be obvious no longer, it is the record-keeping device I tend to fall back on, a kind of biographical point of nativity, the B.C. and A.D. of my private chronology.

I was writing a book at the time. Its merits and deficiencies are irrelevant. *Post hoc ergo propter hoc,* a material fallacy in logic: after this, therefore because of this. Let's not fall victim to that. Let it simply be sufficient to say that the book, which was never published, was ultimately inadequate to the requirements of a decent novel, and very possibly would have been just as inadequate in default of the experience in question. But the book provides an easily accessible illustration of the before and after I'm talking about.

When I returned to the manuscript after the crash, I ignored a reality the significance of which was not as clear to me as it was to my editor, who sensed in my subsequent effort "the will doing the work of the imagination." Had I shared with him the reality I'd confronted after picking up where I'd left off, I might have arrived at the inevitable sooner. Looking back on it, I find it pretty compelling: I won't go so far as to claim that the thirty-two-year-old writer who started that book was unrecognizable to me, but the way he looked at the world was absolutely unrecoverable.

"What a mess *that* was," Mary said, when she and I talked in New York. "You were a hollow person. How do you write a novel if you don't know who you are?"

The book was not a total loss. I've cannibalized it regularly for things I've written since. But its failure was to me the most dramatic proof of how everything was destined to go south. It was a while before I recovered my confidence. What Mary sees as the evidence of a spiritual emptiness is Exhibit A in what Bo Bryan recalls as the void in my professional prospects.

"I remember your house on the Cape," he said, "the first time I walked into it, how it was mainly finished on the outside with the interior still raw, bare plywood and rough drywall. Maybe the house was a metaphor for your career at that stage. Your first book had created a shelter, put a roof over your head and secure walls around you—the house that *Snowblind* built, as Maryanne described it—and nothing on the inside was finished."

My sister Terry remembers the writer who started the book, and says his disappearance was merely temporary. "I would say you were a different person during that time, somewhat humorless, angrier, frightened in a posttraumatic sort of way, and searching for answers. But once you hit bottom—maybe you just got sick of being with yourself—you climbed back up in a remarkable way." She views the dramatic changes as transitory rather than life altering. "You didn't need to learn to appreciate being alive. You appreciated that long before the accident."

I don't know if I can say how the crash changed me, or whether the changes were for the better or the worse. To believe that I was ever entirely carefree is to dream myself into a fantasy. At some point I went from being whoever I was to whoever I am today. The crash is the biographical before and after, but it doesn't in any way define me. It never did. It's part of my story. Would change have come eventually anyway? Does changing so instantly come with a cost? Trying to imagine what might have been is as superlatively sad a prospect as John Greenleaf Whittier famously proclaimed. More than aromatic of old poetry, it smacks of science fiction. How might things have been different had I driven rather than flown to New York that weekend? How analytical can you be?

In the end, you can't really think of yourself as anything but lucky. You just ring it up to circumstance, no more consequential than being caught in the rain. Wrong place, wrong time, just one more interruption of your day.

"Such a random thing to have happened in such a random place," is how Jonathan Ealy put it.

"After a while," Terry recalls, "the only reminder of the accident was the waterbed, so eventually it had to go, too."

Time to get on with life.

And that seems to be what everyone did, as far as I was able to learn—Suzanne, Paul, Brian, Jon—each in his or her own way. Brian, before saying good-bye that day in front of the Brewster Store, told me he felt "no sense of loss." In his survival he saw a "responsibility to value the life you have, to do something with it," he said, to be mindful of "how lucky you are."

"I think we're built to get over things," Kevin Roberts said, the day he and I sat at the beach.

And the opportunity to get over things was ample in the case of the crash. Reminding me that she was a student back then, Suzanne pointed out, "Kids have time."

"I've always been glad that it happened when I was nineteen," Jon told me. "If I'd been older and the same thing happened, I'm sure it would have had a much different impact. At that age I was so used to getting hit playing football, and fooling with adrenaline, that it was just something that happens, you know. My experience was not nearly as horrifying as that of a lot of the others. I was not hurt so badly that I couldn't help out. You always wonder what would happen *if*, and that was one less thing I had to wonder about at that point. 'It happened and now I know how it goes.' "

Certainly, one cannot overlook youth as a factor in the way things eventually played out. In assessing nothing but the survival rate, one has to take account of the fact that the passengers were all relatively young.

(It is harder to know how to account for the fact that of the three passengers treated and released—far less seriously injured than those of us admitted to the hospital—two, Jon and Brian, were not wearing their seat belts, and the other, Suzanne, was belted to a seat that did not remain attached to the airplane. Equally odds-defying is the reality that with three more projectiles loose to fly about the cabin, those who remained in their seats were not more severely injured.)

That most went on to high achievement is probably a function of geography. Families with second homes on the Cape, with children they can afford to fly in, are clearly prosperous if not rich, and prosperous families typically send their kids to college. Of the seven people aboard that night who had not yet started careers, three were in college already, one was in medical school, and the other three summered in Chatham. Jon, before taking his current job, worked as a litigator and corporate lawyer, and if Bob Phillips is right about one of the Chatham sisters, that makes two lawyers and two doctors out of the seven, added to Brian—money being what he does for a living—and Suzanne, who put paid to a career in Manhattan to raise children after marrying a businessman who probably earns more than all of them.

Air New England, with more than 600 employees, some 175 of them pilots, went out of business in October 1981, being unable to weather deregulation of the industry. One of the last of the stand-alone regional airlines, it is gone but not forgotten. Its history is preserved in a plaque that hangs on a wall of the passenger terminal at Barnstable Municipal Airport celebrating the memory of George Parmenter—a reminder to people like me, I guess, that we grade pilots on a pretty tough curve, the aviation community letting us know that if ballplayers were held to a similar standard, there'd be no Hall of Fame.

It would be overly convenient to my story and somewhat melodramatic to suggest that all my life I had been searching for a home. My family might have been transient, but because of the family we were, we never lacked a sense of belonging, never lacked for the comfort and safety that the best of homes provides. And that hasn't changed to this day. Nor can I say that at the time of the crash, I lacked entirely for a sense of community.

It's true that as a child and into my early adulthood, I was a visitor wherever I lived. It always took a while to fit in, even in a place like Boston, the city in which I was born, where my parents before me had also been born, and where all my relatives lived. My accent was wrong when I returned there as a twelve-year-old, and by the time the local accent was once again my own, I was once again on my way, speaking in a manner that would make me an outsider when I arrived at the next port of call. (A couple of years after finishing college I was fired from a Boston newspaper job, and although my employment was terminated for reasons other than the one I was given, I couldn't argue with the city editor when he told me the paper was letting me go because I didn't "know the city." By then I knew Washington better.)

But all of that changed when I got to New York.

At the time, I wasn't really paying attention. I was twenty-five years old, I was passing through town, and I missed my connecting flight north. By the time I got around to rebooking travel, twenty-two years had gone by. I arrived there a young man in a hurry, unable, like many people my age, to distinguish the difference between movement and action. Fearless and full of possibility, I had no plan to speak of, and there was something about the city that said, "I've been waiting here just for you."

Showing up in Manhattan was like walking the flight deck of a carrier. Everyone, it seemed, was from somewhere else, even most of the natives; those who'd been born in the outer boroughs seemed to lay no greater claim to the island than I did. Manhattan is like the navy that way. There is no such thing as an outsider. Yet for all but the truly wealthy of the people I would get to know there, as firmly connected as we felt to New York, there was always the underlying knowledge of the attachment's being in one way temporary. As long as we were young or at least single, we didn't think too hard about the inevitable onset of . . . well . . . let's call it civilian life. My New York friends know what I'm talking about. Many continue to work there, but the number of friends and acquaintances of mine who maintained residency there after they married and started families would fall short of the number of people necessary to field a baseball team. As people departed the city in the interest of putting down roots, the sense of community didn't evaporate, but it became increasingly difficult to discern.

My purchase of property on the Cape was in vague response to their departure and in anticipation more clearly of the day when a one-bedroom apartment, with no closets to speak of and no room for a desk, was going to be of limited utility. As nice as it was—I had the advantage of both house and apartment for the following fifteen years—it was never going to have an attic. Without the house, I would continue through life, as I had done up to then, divesting myself of memory, of everything that didn't fit in a suitcase or on the shelf of an apartment, however cool, in the heart of Greenwich Village. I can't say I was looking for a home, but on the brink of my thirty-third birthday, the firstborn son of a sailor, I had decidedly charted a course in search of something that looked like permanence. And here on the Cape, not far from land's end, is where I came ashore.

The channel that winds through the salt marsh below the house is like an ancient, eternally accurate clock, the hands of which have been sweeping for ages and will continue to sweep long after I'm gone. Reading the movement of the water, as the channel fills and empties, holding it in, now letting it go, you can almost hear the heaving of the moon, breathing in and out. Twice a month come the spring, or swollen, tides, when the sea at flood runs all the way in, overflowing the channel, inundating the marsh. The house sits bayside then. I can switch off the lights, and the full moon, reflected by the water, will cast its glow through the windows, throwing off enough illumination to read by. When the moon is new and out of sight, lingering on the other side of the planet, the stars on nights when the heavens are clear work their own brand of magic in its absence.

Twelve-foot tides are common here at the farthest reaches of the Cape. And they'll go out on you as fast as they come in, ebbing as dramatically as they rise. Navigation can be tricky. When you hear about mass strandings on Cape Cod Bay, the beaching of fifty pilot whales or a dozen white-sided dolphins, marine mammals misreading the migrational charts imprinted in their cellular memory, misreading them or obeying them— maybe getting their magnetic signals crossed—confused, insistent, determined to die, refusing to reverse course . . . When you look at the pictures and see them thrashing, suffocating in the dune grass, lying dead across a dry expanse of sea lavender and high spartina . . . That's where I live. That's my backyard, on a bad day.

At those times when the water is lazy and restricts itself to the channel, coyotes prowl the estuary. They swim as well as the whitetail deer that sometimes appear in the morning, grazing on the wooded banks of the floodplain. On a good day, an entertaining day, great blue herons outnumber the gulls. They stand out there like lawn ornaments, crouching at the edge of the channel, or in it when the tide is low, excellent fishermen, a study in patience, ignoring the burrowing fiddler crabs that scurry at their feet. I watched one of them stalking the marsh one day take a black snake out of the cordgrass. Stretched upright in the vegetation, striking from a height of four feet, it came down on the snake like a javelin. The snake was as long as the bird was tall, and during the fight, it disappeared without ever touching the ground. We get snowy egrets and ospreys, redtails and a lot of marsh hawks, in addition to the songbirds we feed. On ice floes deposited in the winter, harp seals have come in to bask.

The largest animal ever to come within reach of the house was a killer whale. It showed up one day when the weather was nice, and it got hung up in the outer channel. An orca, a meat eater, black and white, the six-ton apex predator you see living out captivity in marine parks, spyhopping and jumping through hoops—it took a few people in a couple of boats over an hour as the tide was receding to herd it back into the bay. There was an outbreak of speculation, dismissed by local biologists, that this characteristically intelligent hunter, a member of the dolphin family, had gotten loose from the navy, which is known to have experimented with training them. A day or so after escaping the marsh, the whale showed up in Provincetown Harbor, accepting snacks thrown by various locals from the end of MacMillan Pier. It hung around there for a couple of days, then headed out into the Atlantic, never to be seen again, leaving town, no doubt, like most visitors—not that they don't return—with the easily won understanding that a little of Provincetown goes a long way.

The cadence of activity on the salt marsh provides a natural ebb and flow to the rhythm of my daily life. Here, the rise and fall of the tide are how the passage of time is measured. And here, twice a day, in defiance of the proverb, time and tide will wait. Twice a day everything hesitates. The clock appears to stop. The tide rushing in, before turning, momentarily pauses. The sea is immobilized between cycles. The moon appears to be holding its breath. And in that brief interval before exhalation, the water stands still, impossibly, as motionless and perfect as glass. Amid the activity there is a moment of equipoise, an instant of perfect balance.

"Emotion recollected in tranquility." It comes down to us from Wordsworth. It's from his preface to the *Lyrical Ballads*. It stipulates a necessary distance between the experience of an event and any reasonable attempt to interpret it. In the immediate upheaval of the senses, the experience defies meaningful expression. Wordsworth was speaking as a poet, not a homicide detective. The distance he was talking about was probably measured in hours. He may have let things cook for as long as a couple of days. It could have been weeks. Or longer. I'm not sure. Thirty years, I think, he would have found a bit extreme. But few poets were more eloquent than Wordsworth on the utility of an instrument that only time can supply—memory— its agency to an author being as indispensable as color to a painter.

Enough time has passed since the night of the crash to invite reasonable interpretation. And in contemplation of the events of that night, what I can say—the best and the worst of it—is that I've struck a kind of balance with them. I've attained a sort of equilibrium. I wouldn't describe it as harmony. Call it an accord. Let's say I've arrived at equipoise.

Within a century of its European settlement, the Cape, its thriving precolonial forests lush with heavy stands of timber, had been stripped of its vegetation. The pine, post oak, American beech, yellow birch, black birch, American holly, hickory, American chestnut, and coastal basswood were gone, and the clearing gave way to so much topsoil loss that Cape Cod, as early as the end of the eighteenth century, was reduced to the sand dunes and salty air that Patti Page would fall in love with 150 years later. By 1850 it was an ecosystem that biologists describe as depauperate, lacking in both the number and variety of species it once supported. The thin surface of the fragile moraine, already vulnerable to wind erosion, now impoverished of nutrients, resisted cultivation, and with the end of the Civil War and the opening of the West to farming, agriculture was largely abandoned, allowing the pioneer species we see today, the pitch pine and the scrub oak, to colonize the abandoned fields. The second-growth forest took hold—more undergrowth, less biodiversity—reaching its peak at about the time Patti Page was topping the charts. In the 1950s, more woodland covered the Cape than at any time since the 1700s.

The trees of the Cape, when the colonists came, were harvested for housing, shipbuilding, and fuel. And one tree that grew in abundance back then was harvested almost exclusively for cash, a tree that had been a staple of trade since before the settlers arrived. It was not religious or political freedom that had enticed the earliest Englishmen to drop anchor on the edge of the primeval forest. It was a tree that had first drawn them here, explorers like Bartholomew Gosnold, the man who is credited with giving Cape Cod its name, and the adventurers who followed him, the first of them sailing under the patronage of Sir Walter Raleigh. They came for a tree, the product of which was as highly prized by Europeans as the spices of the Indies and the incense of Arabia.

They came for the sassafras.

The root and bark of the sassafras, a member of the laurel family, are the source of an essential oil that was used as a fragrance in perfumes and soaps, as a flavoring in candy and root beer, and as the extract necessary, by definition, to the infusion of sassafras tea. Its leaves were dried to make filé powder, the seasoning and thickening agent used when okra was out of season in the preparation of gumbo. But of greatest importance to Europeans in the Age of Discovery were the curative properties sassafras was believed to possess. It was widely used in medicines. Sassafras was considered a wonder drug, an elixir with the power to ward off numerous maladies and cure a variety of others, including venereal disease. One of the first European imports from the New World, sassafras was also one of the more valuable. By the middle of the seventeenth century, it was exceeded as a colonial export to Europe only by tobacco.

"This is one of the only places where sassafras grows in the camp."

The wilderness out of which firefighters carried me that night is still wilderness today, a forest that remains the property of the Boy Scouts, and Bill Monroe, president of the local council, has just led me to the heart of it. Monroe doesn't know it for a fact, he says, but guesses that, at something like a mile square, it is the largest piece of privately owned undeveloped property on the Cape.

There is nothing primeval about the forest. The understory is waist-deep in places, an expanse of bramble, bull brier, wild blueberry, and low-growing laurel that makes walking a straight line impossible. Thrashing through it, here and there, in various parts of the camp, you come across the remnants, now overgrown, of the stone walls that stood over a century ago when the land was given to pasture, evidence of the agriculture that flourished here before the second-growth forest reclaimed the territory.

Such a random thing to have happened in such a random place.

It was across this dense, inhospitable terrain that Suzanne fought her way in the dark before coming upon a trail that night. This is the rough scrub we pushed through moving clear of the wreck, the same underbrush through which firefighters bushwhacked a path to reach us, then carried us out. It is possible that those firefighters, forcing their way into the forest, created the path Monroe and I followed to get here.

"This trail did not exist" back then, says Monroe, who grew up in Centerville and has been hiking these woods since his youth, when he himself was a Boy Scout.

An emergency dispatcher for the Barnstable Fire Department's Centerville-Osterville District, Monroe, forty-seven, the father of three boys who also passed their scouting days here, is spending this weekday in late July the way he frequently spends his day off, taking care of business around the camp. His running across me today, if unexpected, was not unanticipated. Monroe is a veritable picture of the Scout motto, "Be Prepared." From the sturdy soles of his hiking boots to the peak of the baseball cap projected over the lenses of his sunglasses, he is outfitted for a day of orienteering. Around his neck is a red bandana, and circling his waist, cinching the khaki cargo shorts into which his T-shirt is tucked, is a wide leather belt stenciled with the words "2005 National Scout Jamboree." It's a good bet that in at least one of his pockets is a decent magnetic compass.

I was driving home from asking questions at the Yarmouth Fire Department when, without having planned to do so, I skipped the on-ramp to the Mid-Cape Highway and found my way to the camp entrance. I didn't know what I'd run into. Maybe I'd come away with a name, I thought, someone to contact who held some institutional memory of the place. Within fifteen minutes of my arrival, I was introduced to a man by the name of Ed Matthews. Known to the scouts as Uncle Ed, Matthews, who today operates the camp trading post, was a provisional scoutmaster the year of the crash. He was one of two or three people in camp that night, which fell at the end of a staff week preceding the start of programs.

"We heard the plane coming over, [but] we heard them all the time," he told me.

Matthews, with what he wanted me to know were "forty-three years at this camp," had not much to tell me about the crash, but his memory of it seemed clear enough. His reason for having so little to say was probably implicit in the first thing he said when I mentioned it.

"It was a sad thing," he told me, looking away.

I thanked him after spending a few minutes with him, and let him get on with his work. I was standing in the tiny administration building, leaving my number with the helpful woman who'd greeted me as I entered the camp, when Bill Monroe happened to walk in. He and I were introduced, I told him what I was looking for, and Monroe said, "Follow me."

The slope where the sassafras grows is maybe a half a mile from where the trail ended in 1979. The camp has undergone changes since then. To get where Monroe and I are now standing is a hike of no more than a few minutes from what today is the camp athletic field.

"My first recollection of the crash was the newspaper," Monroe is telling me, and he says he remembers asking himself, *Where is that? That's the worst place they could've come down.*

Monroe was nineteen years old that year. For the three years preceding that summer, he had been on the camp staff, but by 1979, having started college and working summers to pay his way through, he was coming by just once a week to say hi.

"I don't think it really affected the program that summer," Monroe says, scouring the slope, "because it was this [remote] part of the camp. This part was used back then for long-range hikes, orienteering class . . ."

Whatever curiosity he had as a teenager did not extend to the presence of the fuselage that for several days lay cordoned off in the woods.

"I didn't," he answers, when I ask if he hiked out to see the wreck. "Actually, for whatever reason, I stayed away. I think I had an uneasy feeling. I remember talking to another kid who was on the staff who hiked in from the other side and came upon it."

The sassafras is growing on the edge of a stretch of narrow pines just below the top of what is known as Prospect Hill. The pines, and the oaks intermixed with them, are smaller, clearly younger than the range of trees sloping away on either side of them. The sassafras is about the same age.

"This is what comes in after you disturb this ground," he says. "Scrub pine. That's the first thing that grows back in. It's the first thing that seems to be able to take root."

After you disturb this ground.

"This is the spot where I have always been led to believe the fuselage lay," he says.

Bob Phillips mentioned this place.

He mentioned it to me at the ballgame and to Monroe sometime before that. While out on the trail with scouts one day, he had come upon this spot. Growing on its border is a tree whose trunk is stripped of its bark in a large, deep, circular scar about fifteen feet off the ground. Catching sight of the damaged tree, Phillips at the time had remarked to himself, as he later told Monroe, "That's probably from the plane crash."

Having been here that night as a firefighter, the night the trail had first been cut, Phillips would have been in a position to know.

"I can't think what else would have caused it," Monroe says, seeing it now for the first time. "Up that high . . . It was never in a place where a Boy Scout with a hatchet could have cut it. That's something large that . . ."

He pauses for several seconds.

"That's something large," he says, "that cut that tree."

With regularity, all the time we've been out here, the roar of incoming aircraft has punctuated the conversation. They've been erupting in on us overhead, airplanes skimming the tree-tops, so low you can count the rivets, drowning out our words, vectored in on final approach to runway 24 at Barnstable, two and a half miles to the southwest.

What scoutmasters announce as airplane breaks, around campfires or during class, are a frequent occurrence in the camp. They are observed with regularity, whenever a plane comes over. "If a guy just keeps talking," Monroe explains, "you've lost thirty seconds of whatever it was he was saying." Such breaks, he tells me, were common when he himself was a scout. "You'd hear it coming, and he'd say, 'Plane break!' and he'd fold his arms and he'd wait for it to go by and then continue as if nothing ever happened. The eerie thing of it is, as a kid, being in camp on a foggy day, you couldn't see anything, but you could hear it. The ceiling comes in very, very low."

I can imagine the ceiling coming in as he says it.

I remember lying here twenty-eight years ago. I remember being unable to see anything. I can remember how, here in the night, in the stillness of the forest, the eldest of the three sisters slipped in and out of consciousness, screaming, how she screamed when the power to the emergency light died and the doorway of the downed airplane, the only source of illumination, went dark, how at that moment, the impenetrable, fog-shrouded night went from bewildering to immaculate black.

Once we'd escaped the airplane, terror gave way to a certain sense of relief, but it never really departed the field. I remember lying still, adrenaline pumping, wondering if they knew we were down. It wasn't a question of whether they'd find us, but how long it would take them to do it, and how many of us would be alive when they did. How many would be alive when dawn broke? Here we lay twenty-eight years ago, we lay here for over an hour, though it seemed longer than that. I remember little of how the time passed. And the things I remember are among those things I continually have to remind myself to forget.

Quite a thing, as someone said, for a summer evening on the Cape.

Monroe and I are making our way back to the trail when he tells me about the stories. Here, on foggy nights, he says, in the dark shadows around flickering campfires, one of the ghost stories that animate the bedtime hours is the mysterious tale of a plane that crashed, vanishing one midnight long ago, deep in the deserted forest.

Monroe is careful to add that he cannot attest to the details.

"I've been told that people tell the story, but haven't heard it told."

I try to imagine how the story is told, wonder what it would be like to hear it. I wonder if it changes in the retelling. It has been passed down as part of the folklore, and summer-to-summer, turning in on itself, it has entered the realm of the apocryphal. Here, where they happened, the events of that night are enveloped in the mist of legend. Here, on this ground that has been disturbed, the sassafras, beginning its rebirth on the Cape, stands in witness to a strange reciprocity. This place that haunts our memory is now the shadowland of a children's fairy tale, and we upon whom its horrors were visited are the ghosts by which it is haunted.

I first heard mention of the stories before I met Monroe, when I stopped by the camp some months earlier, curious as to whether it was still in use and, if so, whether those who used it had any knowledge of the crash. The season had ended, and I was talking to the young ranger in residence, an Eagle Scout attending the community college. He looked to be just out of his teens. And he was as curious as I.

"They say one night, a long time ago, a girl walked down through here who crashed in a plane. Is that the one?" he asked.

"That's the one," I said.

"It's a story they tell."

"It's a true story."

"It really happened?"

In the half a lifetime that had passed, it was a question I sometimes asked myself.

Yes, I told him. The girl and everything. Just like they tell it in the story.

"Once upon a time," I said.

ACKNOWLEDGMENTS

I could not have written this book without the cooperation of the numerous people whose names appear in its pages. I thank them for their generosity and for the time and effort they dedicated to helping me tell the story, with special thanks to the members of my family and to those survivors of the crash who came forward to help me reconstruct the incident and the events surrounding it. My fellow survivors, in leading me to an understanding of its aftermath, were as courageous in sharing their personal stories as they were in risking their lives to save others on the night of the tragedy. I am especially grateful to Suzanne Mourad. Her unqualified offer of help at the outset made the undertaking possible, and her advice and encouragement along the way were instrumental in my following the story to the end. For their cooperation, their support, their help in the preparation of the manuscript, or for other personal and professional contributions to the success of the project, I am indebted to: Jessica Almon, Alan Bowles, Marjorie Braman, Jamie Byng, Beverly Callistini, Patrick Cavanaugh, Norma Holmes, Gip Hoppe, John Kalell, Robert LaPointe, Russ Maguire, Jay Mandel, Marianne McCaffery, Anjali Mecklai, Tim Miller, Sara Nelson, Elizabeth Parker, Ed Ramey, Eric Rayman, Jim Regan, Sandie Riley, Jamie Saul, Elizabeth Sheinkman, Randall Sherman, Danny Silverman, Gary Stimeling, Susan Stinson, Steve Sullivan, and Charles M. Young. Special acknowledgment for their efforts is due Vincent Amicosante, who showed up at the game early and stayed late, and tireless Philip Richardson, who, in typical fashion, played his best hand when the stakes got really interesting.

This book in all the important ways really belongs to Jennifer Walsh. She has been steering me in its direction for more than a decade. I didn't know I needed to tell the story until she made it impossible not to. Her belief in it and her patience were an expression of a belief in me that, from the day she agreed to represent me, has motivated my belief in myself, and this book, more than any other, was her way of making me prove it. Among the blessings she conferred on the book was her placing it in the hands of as fine an editor as a writer could hope to work with. I have been fortunate to collaborate with many excellent editors over the years; if my luck holds out, there will be others, and all of them will be Wendy Wolf. Writing a book is difficult under the best of conditions. Writing a book like this one is like writing every word in the dark. The only thing more extravagant than the degree to which she improved it is the manner in which she made every aspect of bringing it to light enjoyable. Delivering the book would have been a more daunting and far more doubtful prospect were it not for the help of Jeff Blanchard, the one friend I trusted to read the manuscript in the course of its being written. As talented an editor as he is a writer and reporter, he was a consistent source of enthusiasm, wisdom and professional guidance. He followed the progress of the book from its inception, always there to push it in the right direction, inexhaustible in providing advice on how to push it further. Were it not for Patricia Riley, to whom this book is dedicated, there would have been little to dignify the effort.